The Thames

www.getmapping.com

from source to sea

by Ian Harrison

First published in 2004 by
HarperCollinsPublishers
77-85 Fulham Palace Road
London W6 8JB

The Collins website address is:
www.collins.co.uk

Collins is a registered trademark of HarperCollins Publishers

Photography © 2004 Getmapping plc

Getmapping plc hereby asserts its moral right to be identified as the author of this work

Getmapping can produce an individual print of any area shown in this book, or of any area within the
United Kingdom. The image can be centred wherever you choose, printed at any size from A6 to 7.5
metres square, and at any scale up to 1:1,000. For further information, please contact Getmapping
on 0845 0551550, or log on to www.getmapping.com

A CIP catalogue record for this book is available from the British Library.

ISBN: 0 00 716211 1

Atlas devised for Collins by Martin Brown
Design: Colin Brown

Colour origination by Colourscan, Singapore
Printed and bound by Editoriale Johnson, Italy

Index: Chris Howes
Proofreading: Margaret Gilbey

All distances given are approximate and should not be relied upon as a precise measurement
The photographic representation of rivers and canals is no evidence of navigable passage, nor does
the inclusion of navigational information imply any right of navigation

CONTENTS

FOREWORD

The Thames: from source to sea, is unquestionably a superb photographic map of the Thames, but it is also much more than that. It is a celebration of England's longest and greatest river – part history, part navigational handbook, part literary companion and part tourist guide.

In charting the course of the Thames the full 215 miles from the source to the sea, this photographic atlas tells the fascinating story of a river that was aptly described by 19th century MP John Burns as 'liquid history'. The Thames flowed across England long before people existed to name it, and its banks have yielded the oldest human artefacts to be found in Britain, some quarter of a million years old. Eventually it was given Britain's second oldest documented place name, recorded for the first time in the account of Julius Caesar's invasion, c. 55 BC, as **Tamesis**. Since then, although the nature of its importance has changed, the Thames has continued to act as one of the country's vital arteries and as the lifeblood of the capital.

Following the stripling Thames as it flows eastward from its disputed but official source in the Cotswolds, as it swells into majestic maturity and flows into the North Sea, this book tells the story not only of the physical changes that take place along the 200-plus miles of the river's course, but also of the historic changes that have taken place in the 2,000-plus years since its name was first recorded. Geographically, the Thames is a lowland river flowing lazily through a gentle landscape of watermeadows and woodland, the only significant contrast being the steep, wooded hills of the Goring Gap, near Reading, where it carved a new course through the chalk during the last ice age. Historically, the changes are, not surprisingly, far greater: although people still fish in the Thames it is no longer a significant source of food; although industry still uses its water, it is no longer a source of power for mills; although people still travel on the Thames, it is no longer a vital communications link – that role is now fulfilled by the road and rail links that shadow the course of the Thames and also appear in this atlas; the M4 and the erstwhile Great Western Railway.

The story of the changing river is told in four distinct sections: from the source to Oxford, from Oxford to Reading, from Reading to Teddington, and from Teddington to the sea. The first section sees the river grow from a barely visible valley, dry for most of the year, into a fully fledged river, and includes such landmarks as Cricklade (where the right of navigation begins), Lechlade (site of the highest lock on the river and the practical limit of navigation for most craft), and the junction of the river with the Oxford Canal, which from 1790 linked the Thames with the midlands. From Oxford to Reading the isolated, expansive flood plain that characterised the first section is gradually filled by an increasing number of towns and villages, many of them, such as Abingdon, Dorchester, and Wallingford, dating back to prehistoric times. Section Three takes in Henley with its famous regatta, Stanley Spencer's Cookham, royal Windsor, and historic Runnymede, where the Magna Carta was sealed. The final section of this unique atlas begins at Teddington, whose lock marks the upper limit of the tidal Thames, and from here the mature river flows through the capital, beneath the city's famous bridges, past the Tower of London, beyond the Thames Barrier and out to sea.

The Thames: from source to sea performs several functions as it follows the river along its course. It tells the stories of the people who lived and worked on or near the Thames, the pubs and churches that line its banks, the architects who designed its bridges, the historic events that have taken place in its valley, and the artists, poets and writers who have been inspired by its scenery. It also acts as a navigational aid for those boating on the river, a walking guide for those using the Thames Path, and a tourist guide for those visiting the towns and cities along the way. Symbols show the location of watering points (W) and moorings (M) for those travelling the river by boat, and the heights of the bridges, the rise of the locks and the locations of the weirs are also given. The book describes the approximate course of the Thames Path, which was officially declared a National Trail in 1989 and was the first such trail to follow a river for what the Countryside Agency claims to be its entire length. (In fact the path covers 180 miles, from the source to the Thames Barrier, beyond which the Thames could arguably be said to be an estuary rather than a river.) For most of the stretch between Lechlade and the flood barrier, the Thames Path follows what was once the river's towpath, although it occasionally has to deviate due to the intransigence of private landowners. Fourthly, in addition to the stories, the navigational notes and a guide to the Thames Path, the book is interspersed with spreads in which the river makes only a passing appearance, providing a closer view of tourist attractions such as Oxford, Mapledurham, Cliveden, Hampton Court and Greenwich. And for any boaters, walkers or tourists requiring liquid refreshment with their liquid history, the all important Thames pubs are marked with a 🍺.

For all its history as a vital resource for trade, industry, transport and communication, the Thames now plays an important role as a source of pleasure and recreation, something which was first officially recognised in the Thames Preservation Act of 1885. The Act stated that the Thames 'has largely come to be used as a place of public recreation and resort: and that it is expedient that provision should be made that it should be preserved as a place of regulated public recreation'. It is an important point, but lacks the joie de vivre of Kenneth Grahame, author of '**The Wind in the Willows**', who wrote of boating on the Thames that: 'Believe me, my young friend, there is nothing – absolutely nothing – half so much worth doing as simply messing about in boats.' Or those who prefer to remain on the bank could follow in the steps of Edmund Spenser, who 'Walkt forth to ease my payne along the shoare of silver streaming Themmes,' and continued with the refrain: 'Sweete Themmes! runne softly, till I end my Song'.

Enjoy the river.

Ian Harrison

THE THAMES (FROM SOURCE TO SEA)

Distance: 215 miles (344 Kilometres)

Symbols used within the atlas;

M	overnight mooring. Usually indicated on river navigations, where mooring is restricted. There may be a charge.
W	water point
S	sewage or 'elsan' disposal point
R	refuse disposal point
🍺	public house (within vicinity of the river)

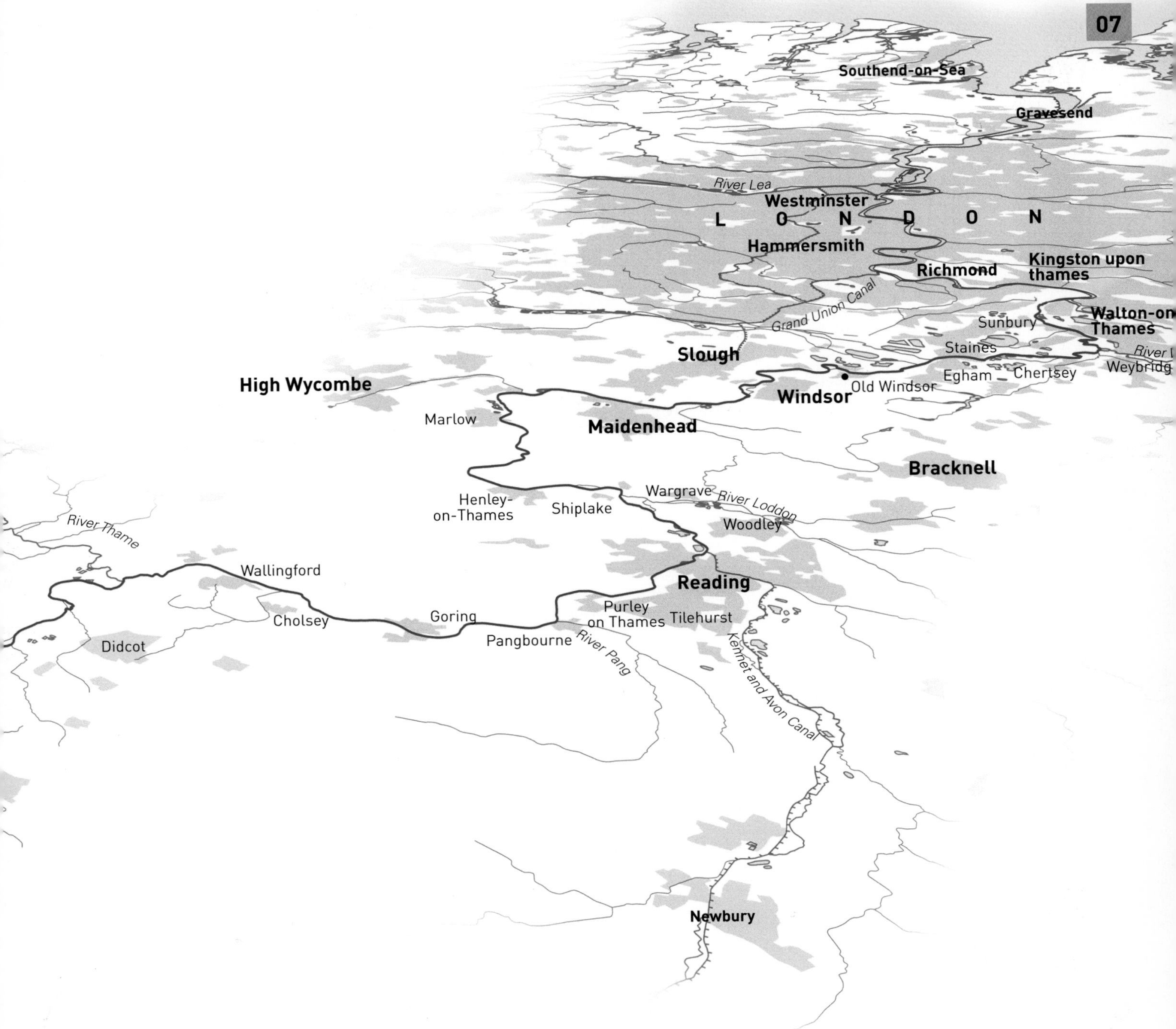

Southend-on-Sea

Gravesend

River Lea

Westminster

L O N D O N

Hammersmith

Richmond

Kingston upon thames

Grand Union Canal

Sunbury

Walton-on Thames

Slough

Staines

River Weybridg

Egham

Chertsey

Windsor

Old Windsor

High Wycombe

Bracknell

Marlow

Maidenhead

Wargrave

River Loddon

Henley-on-Thames

Shiplake

Woodley

River Thame

Wallingford

Reading

Goring

Purley on Thames

Tilehurst

Cholsey

Pangbourne

River Pang

Kennet and Avon Canal

Didcot

Newbury

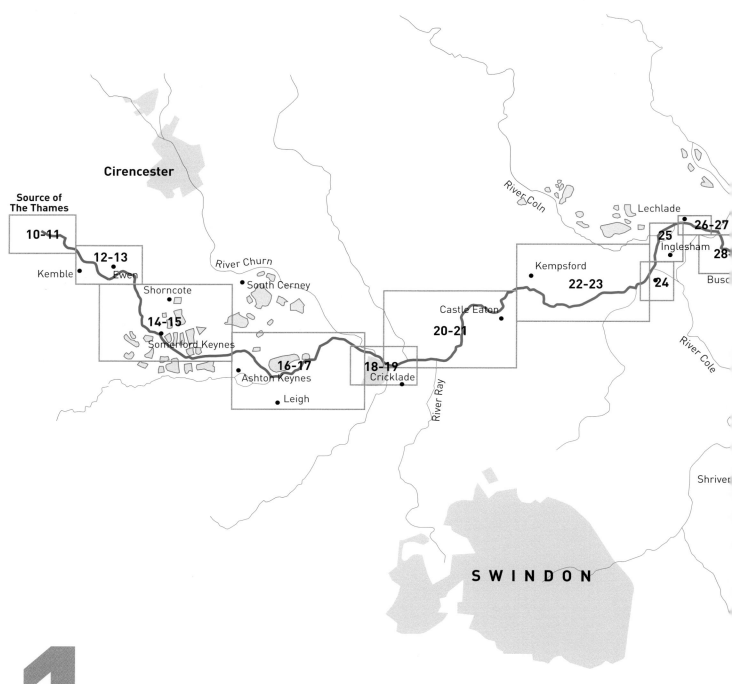

Cirencester

Source of
The Thames

10-11

12-13

Kemble

Ewen

Shorncote

River Churn

South Cerney

14-15

Somerford Keynes

16-17

Ashton Keynes

Leigh

18-19

Cricklade

20-21

River Ray

Castle Eaton

Kempsford

22-23

River Coln

Lechlade

26-27

25

Inglesham

24

28

Busc

River Cole

Shriver

S W I N D O N

1

SOURCE TO OXFORD

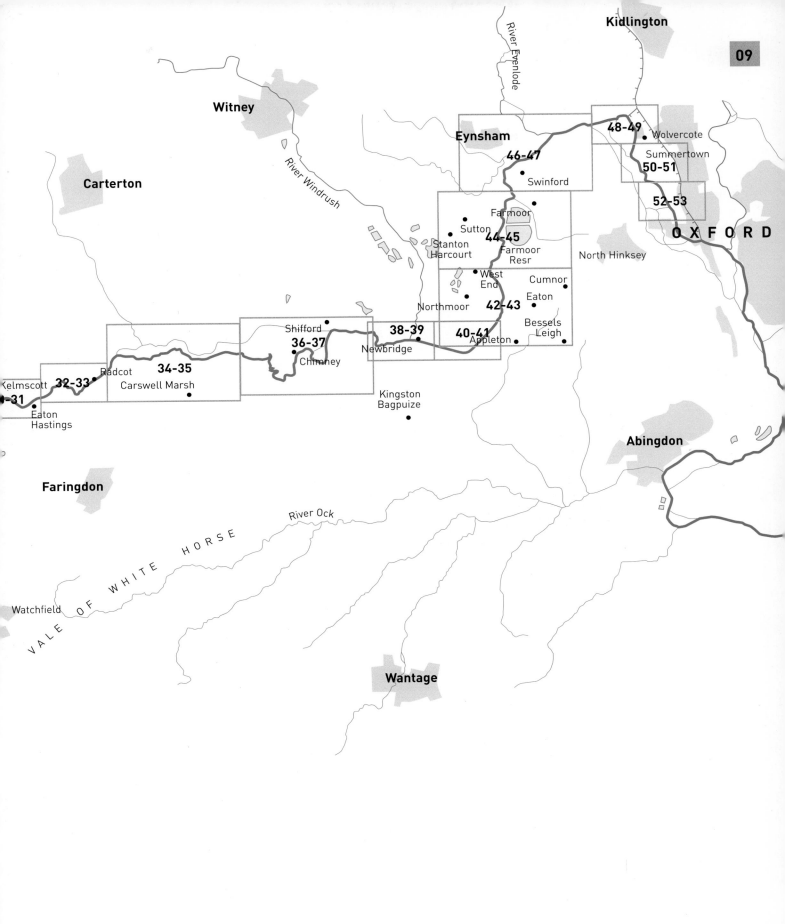

Kidlington

Witney

Carterton

Eynsham

46-47

48-49 Wolvercote

Summertown

50-51

Swinford

52-53

Farmoor

Sutton

44-45

Stanton
Harcourt

Farmoor
Resr

North Hinksey

O X F O R D

West
End

Cumnor

Eaton

42-43

Northmoor

Shifford

38-39

40-41

Bessels
Leigh

Appleton

36-37

Newbridge

Chimney

Radcot

34-35

Kingston
Bagpuize

Kelmscott **32-33**

Carswell Marsh

-31

Eaton
Hastings

Faringdon

River Windrush

River Evenlode

River Ock

V A L E   O F   W H I T E   H O R S E

Watchfield

Abingdon

Wantage

trewsbury camp
Iron age hill fort of about 17 acres

source of the thames
A simple stone monument beneath an ash tree reads: 'The Conservation of the River Thames 1857–1974. This stone was placed here to mark the source of the River Thames.' In front of the monument is a small basin of stones where the head spring of the Thames occasionally bubbles to the surface.

site of medieval village of hullasey

fosse way
The Roman road from Exeter and Bath (south-west of here) to Cirencester, Leicester and Lincoln (to the north east).

SOURCE OF THE THAMES

Distance: 0.7 miles (1.1 kilometres)

Thames path: Southwards from the spring, crossing the Fosse Way and continuing towards Kemble village.

Scale 1:6,250

ALTERNATIVE SOURCE?

The official source of the Thames is the spring close to Thames Head but some people claim that the true source is Seven Springs, north of Cirencester. They argue that the River Churn, which rises at Seven Springs, is not a tributary of the Thames but is in fact the Thames itself, because it rises further inland than the official source, almost twice as high above sea level, and rarely dries up. In 1937 Mr Perkins, MP for Stroud, asked the Minister for Agriculture to transfer recognition of the official source to Seven Springs, which was in Mr Perkins's constituency, but the request was refused.

A 433

thames head bridge

thames & severn canal (disused)
Opened in 1789 to link London and Bristol, the canal left the Thames near Lechlade and cut across Gloucestershire to the Severn Estuary, often running close to the river, as here. It was closed in 1927.

12

11
up stream

disused railway

K E M B L E

parker's
bridge

Scale 1:6,250

lyd well

Lyd Well, which means 'loud spring', is mentioned in the Domesday Book. This ancient spring is often the first place where water can be seen in the course of the nascent Thames.

severall's copse

KEMBLE TO EWEN

Distance: 1.9 miles (3.05 kilometres)

Thames path: Southwards from Lyd Well, crossing the A429 and bearing left at Parker's Bridge into the village of Ewen.

kemble

The river skirts Kemble, so there is some argument as to whether Kemble (opposite page) or Ewen is truly 'the first village on the Thames'. Kemble boasts an Early English-style church dating from 1679, dedicated to All Saints, whose 120-ft steeple is a landmark for those walking the Thames path

ewen

Arguably the first village on the Thames, depending on whether or not Kemble is defined as being 'on the Thames' or skirted by it.

mill farm

The farm stands on the site of Ewen Mill, which was the highest water-mill on the Thames until it was dismantled. The mill was described in the 1850s as being 'sufficiently rude in character to be picturesque'.

wild duck inn

This atmospheric and, supposedly, haunted inn occupies a converted Cotswold stone barn built in 1563. The à la carte menu includes duck dishes, and the anatrine theme is continued with the house beer, Duck Pond Bitter.

E W E N

MILLS

Until the 20th century, mills were an important part of life on the river and the local miller would have been a man of some influence, using sluices to regulate the flow of the river through the mill stream and also controlling river traffic through the mill weir, often charging hefty tolls for allowing barges to pass. The number of farms named after mills along this section of the Thames is evidence of just how many mills there once were.

upper mill farm

old mill farm

POOLE KEYNES

kemble mill

somerford lakes reserve
Part of the Cotswold Water Park

neigh bridge country park
Part of the Cotswold Water Park. In dry weather the lake within Neigh Bridge Country Park is often the first sight of water for those following the course of the Thames from its source.

EWEN TO FURZE BRAKE

Distance: 3.4 miles (5.4 kilometres)

Thames path: Southwards from Ewen, skirting Somerford Keynes and bearing east between the lakes towards Ashton Keynes.

Scale 1:12,500

baker's arms
The pub dates from the 16th century and now incorporates what was once the village shop.

keynes country park
Part of Britain's largest water park, the Cotswold Water Park. Leisure facilities include a bathing beach, cafés, boat and cycle hire, basketball courts, barbecues, angling and themed children's play areas. There is also a Millennium Park Centre housed in an ecologically designed oak building heated and cooled by lake energy.

cotswold community

SOMERFORD KEYNES

furze brake
Part of the Cotswold Water Park

lower mill farm

16 down stream

15
up stream

9697

ASHTON
KEYNES

holy cross church
There were no less than four preaching
crosses in Ashton Keynes, hence the
dedication of the church to the Holy Cross.

white hart
Originally the Cordwainer's Arms, in honour
of the local trade of shoemaking, the
White Hart was built c.1750.

ashton keynes
The river divides into several streams
through Ashton Keynes, one of them
running parallel to the main street, before
leaving the village strengthened by the
addition of the Swill Brook tributary.

Scale 1:12,500

18
down stream

hailstone hill

north wiltshire canal (disused)
At one time the North Wiltshire Canal linked the Thames & Severn Canal (to the north) with the Wilts & Berks Canal (to the south), and was carried across the Thames here by the Latton Aqueduct, which was opened in 1819. The canal is now disused and the aqueduct has been replaced by a wooden footbridge.

bournelake farm bridge

cleveland lakes
Another part of the extensive Cotswold Water Park

ASHTON KEYNES TO HAILSTONE HILL

Distance: 5.5 miles (8.8 kilometres)
Thames path: Through Ashton Keynes, bearing south-east across the gravel workings and then around the lakes towards Hailstone Hill.

CRICKLADE

st sampson's church
The massive tower of St Sampson's was
added to the existing church after the
Reformation by John Dudley, Duke of
Northumberland and Earl of Warwick, who
is more famous for trying to secure the
succession to the throne for his daughter-
in-law Lady Jane Grey – both were
beheaded for their trouble.

Scale 1:6,250

CRICKLADE

**Distance: 1.3 miles
(2.1 kilometres)
Thames path:** South-east across
North Meadow towards Cricklade,
skirting the northern edge of the
town and continuing eastwards
under Ermine Street (A419).

north meadow
An ancient meadow still preserved as
Lammas Land, North Meadow was
established as a nature reserve in 1973
and is famous for springtime displays of
snake's head fritillary.

ermine street
The A419 Cricklade by-pass was built on
the route of the ancient Roman road of
Ermine Street, or Ermin Way.

river churn
The River Churn, which has a rival claim
to be the source of the Thames (see
p.11), joins the Thames as a tributary at
Cricklade.

high bridge
Also known as the Town Bridge

st mary's church
A Norman church which has been
rededicated as Cricklade's Roman
Catholic church.

cricklade
Charles Dickens's son Charles
described Cricklade in 1888 as 'a
pleasant little town, clean and
well-paved, but [it] has not been the
scene of any particularly remarkable
events since it suffered the fate of so
many of the other Thames towns and
was plundered by the Danes in 1015'.
The right of navigation begins at
Cricklade, though few craft venture
further than Lechlade, further
downstream.

river key

20
down stream

CRICKLADE TO CASTLE EATON

Distance: 5.0 miles (8.0 kilometres)

Thames path: Eastwards out of Cricklade, passing beneath Ermine
Street (A419) and following the Thames north-eastwards before
leaving the river to follow the road through Castle Eaton.

thames & severn canal (disused)
Opened in 1789 to link London and Bristol,
the canal left the Thames near Lechlade
and cut across Gloucestershire to the
Severn Estuary, often running close to the
river, as here. It was closed in 1927.

EYSEY

water eaton footbridge

eysey footbridge

A419

19
up stream

CRICKLADE

river ray
Tributary with its source near Swindon

Scale 1:12,500

castle eaton bridge
A Victorian bridge which, being made of iron, has been described as being 'more appropriate to a railway than to a river'.

st mary's church
The church was restored by architect William Butterfield during the 1860s, at which time he added a distinctive bell-turret and spire to the roof of the nave.

C A S T L E
E A T O N

red lion
This is the first pub on the course of the Thames that actually stands on the bank of the river. The Red Lion is renowned for traditional bar games including crib, table skittles and shove ha'penny, and it is also the home of the Castle Eaton Pétanque Club.

plague cottages
A plaque commemorates the fact that these cottages were preserved from 'the fatal cattle plague of 1866'.

water eaton house
William Morris, founder of the Society for the Protection of Ancient Buildings, was clearly impressed with Water Eaton House. In 1871 he wrote of Kelmscott Manor (which he was considering leasing as a country retreat for his family) that it was 'heaven on earth; an old stone house like Water Eaton, and such a garden close down on the river ...'

fairford airfield
Part of Fairford Airfield, which opened in 1944 under the control of RAF Bomber Command but was almost immediately transferred to Transport Command, whose gliders played an important role over Normandy and Arnhem. The airfield currently hosts the annual Royal International Air Tattoo each July on behalf of the RAF Benevolent Fund.

KEMPSFORD

axe & compass
The Axe & Compass was created during the 19th century by knocking together three 15th-century cottages.

21 up stream

blackford lane

blackford farm

kempsford
Kempsford was once the home of John of Gaunt, Duke of Lancaster, whose castle stood on the riverside close to what is now the vicarage. Chaucer was a friend of the Lancasters and wrote 'The Book of the Duchesse' in memory of Gaunt's wife Lady Blanche, who died in 1369. It is thought that some of Chaucer's poetry may have been written at Kempsford –
'The Parliament of Fowls'
certainly captures the atmosphere:

'A garden saw I ful of blosmy bowes
Upon a ryver, in a grene mede,
There as swetnesse evermore inow is,
With flowres white, blewe, yelwe,
and rede.'

the george
The pub sign is a portrait of George I, so it seems that the George is named not after England's patron saint but after the country's first Hanoverian king, during whose reign it was built. The pub also has a connection with George's descendant George IV, because from 1816 it was leased from local landowner Colonel George Hanger, Lord Coleraine. Coleraine lived beyond his means as part of the Prince Regent's social circle, and found himself in such debt that he had to demolish Kempsford manor house and sell the materials. The Prince Regent was crowned George IV in 1821, and Coleraine died three years later in 1824.

church of st mary the virgin
The superb Perpendicular tower of Kempsford's Church of St Mary the Virgin was built in 1390 at the behest of John of Gaunt to commemorate his late wife, Lady Blanche. Nine years later, their son was crowned Henry IV.

Scale 1:12,500

thames & severn canal (disused)
Another stretch of the disused Thames & Severn Canal. In the late
18th and early 19th centuries a large number of canals were dug
because they were easier, quicker and cheaper to navigate than the
river. So many were built that the Thames Commissioners urged
people to 'unite in resisting the confederacy and conspiracy against
Old Father Thames'. What they meant, of course, was the
confederacy and conspiracy against the profits to be derived from
charging tolls to river traffic.

24
down stream

brazen church hill

KEMPSFORD TO INGLESHAM

Distance: 4.5 miles (7.3 kilometres)
Thames path: Eastwards along Blackford Lane, turning left to rejoin
the Thames just north of Blackford Farm before leaving the river
again at Hannington Bridge and following the bridle-path into the
parish of Inglesham.

hannington bridge
Evidence of an earlier Roman bridge was
found while dredging the river close to the
present Hannington Bridge.

river cole

A 361

UPPER
INGLESHAM

Scale 1:6,250

UPPER INGLESHAM

**Distance: 0.9 miles
(1.5 kilometres)
Thames path: Northwards
along the A361 from Upper
Inglesham.**

WHAT'S IN A NAME?

'Thames' is the oldest documented place name in British history after Kent, having been first recorded, in the account of Julius Caesar's invasion c. 55 BC, as **'Tamesis'**. There are various theories as to the meaning of the name, including 'the river,' 'the dark one,' 'dark water,' and 'the broad Isis,' where Isis is considered to be a variation of esk, ouse and uisge, which all mean water. (Whisky takes its name from uisge beatha, meaning water of life.) In places, the Thames is known as the Isis, and in his poem 'Windsor Forest', Alexander Pope makes reference to **'the famed authors of his ancient name'**:

'Around his throne the sea-born
brothers stood,
Who swell with tributary urns his flood,
First the famed authors of his
ancient name,
The winding Isis and the
fruitful Thame!'

INGLESHAM TO LECHLADE

Distance: 1.2 miles (2.0 kilometres)

Thames path: Left off the A361 towards Inglesham, then leaving the road to follow the course of the river into Lechlade.

LECHLADE

riverside park

INGLESHAM

river coln
Tributary rising high up in the Cotswolds

round house
Round houses were built as accommodation for the Thames & Severn Canal lock-keepers, and several have survived the canal, which closed in 1927. The Round House marks the usual limit of the navigable Thames for powered craft, though the actual right of navigation begins and ends further upstream at Cricklade.

thames & severn canal (disused)
The canal, opened in 1789, left the Thames here, close to what is now Roundhouse Farm. Opposite the farm are the remains of a bridge that once carried the towpath across the river, from which point it became a canal towpath rather than a river towpath. For those following the river downstream, the towpath from here onwards takes on the role of the Thames Path.

church of st john the baptist
A 13th-century church rescued by William Morris from the Gothic excesses of Victorian restoration, and now preserved by the Churches Conservation Trust.

Scale 1:6,250

L E C H L A D E

25 up stream

M

M

ha'penny bridge
So called because of
the toll that was once
charged for crossing
the bridge.
15'6"

st lawrence's church
Shelley wrote his 'Stanzas in a Summer
Evening Churchyard' here in 1815 after seeing
St Lawrence's at sunset, and the verses are
quoted in a plaque which was set into the
churchyard wall in 1968:

'Clothing in hues of Heaven thy
dim and distant spire,
Around whose lessening and invisible height
Gather among the stars the clouds of night.'

st john's bridge
The bridge and the lock take their
name from St John's Priory,
established at Lechlade in 1250 and
dissolved by Edward IV in 1472.
13'10"

Scale 1:3,125

LECHLADE

Distance: 0.8 miles (1.25 kilometres)
Thames path: Following the towpath eastwards out of Lechlade on the south bank of the river.

lechlade

Shelley, Mary Godwin, Thomas Love Peacock and Charles Clairmont stayed at the New Inn Hotel in Lechlade after rowing here from Windsor in 1815. Charles Dickens Jr also enjoyed the New Inn, but complained that 'the ideas of the inhabitants on the subject of paving are, it may be remarked, open to considerable exception'.

st john's lock

The highest lock on the river. A well-travelled statue of Old Father Thames reclines in front of the lock house, having been commissioned in 1854 for the Crystal Palace, moved to the source of the river at Thames Head and finally brought here, close to the start of the navigable Thames.
2'10"

trout inn

Another Lechlade landmark with connections to St John's Priory, until 1704 the Trout Inn was known as Ye Signe of St John Baptist Head, and the building was originally an almshouse of the priory. The pub hosts a number of annual events including a National Music Festival, a jazz festival, a folk festival, and a Tractor and Steam Rally.

st john's bridge

trout inn

st john's lock
R S

down stream
28

27
up stream

river leach
Tributary also known as the Lech, from which Lechlade takes its name.

bloomers hole footbridge

st mary's church
Norman church with windows by Sir Edwa
Burne-Jones. Next door is the beautiful
Old Parsonage, built in 1703.

M

PILLBOXES
Along this stretch of the riverside are a
number of concrete 'pillboxes', built in
1940 to fortify the natural boundary of
the river as a last-ditch defence to
repel any invading forces. Thankfully
these pillboxes were never put to the
test, and now languish by the river as a
reminder of the Second World War.

B U S C O T

Scale 1:6,250

ST JOHN'S BRIDGE TOWARDS KELMSCOTT

Distance: 2.4 miles (3.9 kilometres)

Thames path: South bank to Bloomers Hole, over the footbridge and continuing on the north bank towards Kelmscott.

brandy island

When Australian gold trader Robert Campbell bought Buscot Park in 1859, he initiated a programme of agricultural industrialisation that included irrigation schemes and a narrow-gauge railway running round the estate. He also built a distillery on this river island for making spirit from sugar beet, hence the name Brandy Island.

buscot lock
5'7"

30
down stream

buscot estate

Ernest Cook bequeathed the Buscot and Coleshill estates to the National Trust in 1956, a total of 7,500 acres including the country house of Buscot Park (out of picture), and the villages of Buscot, Coleshill (out of picture) and Eaton Hastings (p.31). The Faringdon Collection at Buscot Park includes paintings by Murillo, Rembrandt, Gainsborough, Reynolds, Rossetti, Madox Brown and Sir Edward Burne-Jones and furniture by Robert Adam and Thomas Hope.

THAMES QUOTATIONS

William Morris, craftsman, poet, painter and a member of the Pre-Raphaelite Brotherhood, lived at Kelmscott Manor and loved this stretch of the Thames. In his poem 'The Earthly Paradise' he dreamt that the banks of the Thames in London could be as idyllic as at Kelmscott:

Forget six counties overhung with smoke,
Forget the snorting steam and piston stroke,
Forget the spreading of the hideous town;
Think rather of the pack-horse on the down,
And dream of London, small and white and clean,
The clear Thames bordered by its gardens green

K E L M S C O T T

eaton weir

A small footbridge (9'9") marks the site of a flash weir that no longer exists, having been taken up in 1936 (for explanation of flash weir see p.35, 'Rushey Lock'). Eaton Weir is sometimes known as Hart's Weir, after the family that kept it for more than a century.

M

kelmscott manor

The country home of William Morris for 25 years and now owned by the Society of Antiquaries. Morris rented Kelmscott Manor from 1871 until his death in 1896, after which his wife retired there and bought the house. When he first saw Kelmscott Manor, Morris described it as 'a heaven on earth ... such a garden close down on the river, a boat house and all things handy. I am going down there again on Saturday with Rossetti and my wife: Rossetti because of sharing it with us if the thing looks likely'. Rossetti was not so taken with Kelmscott, nor Kelmscott with Rossetti, and the painter gave up his share of the lease in 1874.

29 up stream

Scale 1:6,250

st george's church
William Morris died in Hammersmith but he was buried in St George's Church, close to his beloved Kelmscott Manor. His tomb was designed by his friend, the architect and designer Philip Webb.

plough inn
Built in 1631, the Plough reopened in 1993 after modernisation but fortunately retained much of its character, including oak beams and flagstone floors.

eaton hastings church

M

M

32
down stream

EATON
HASTINGS

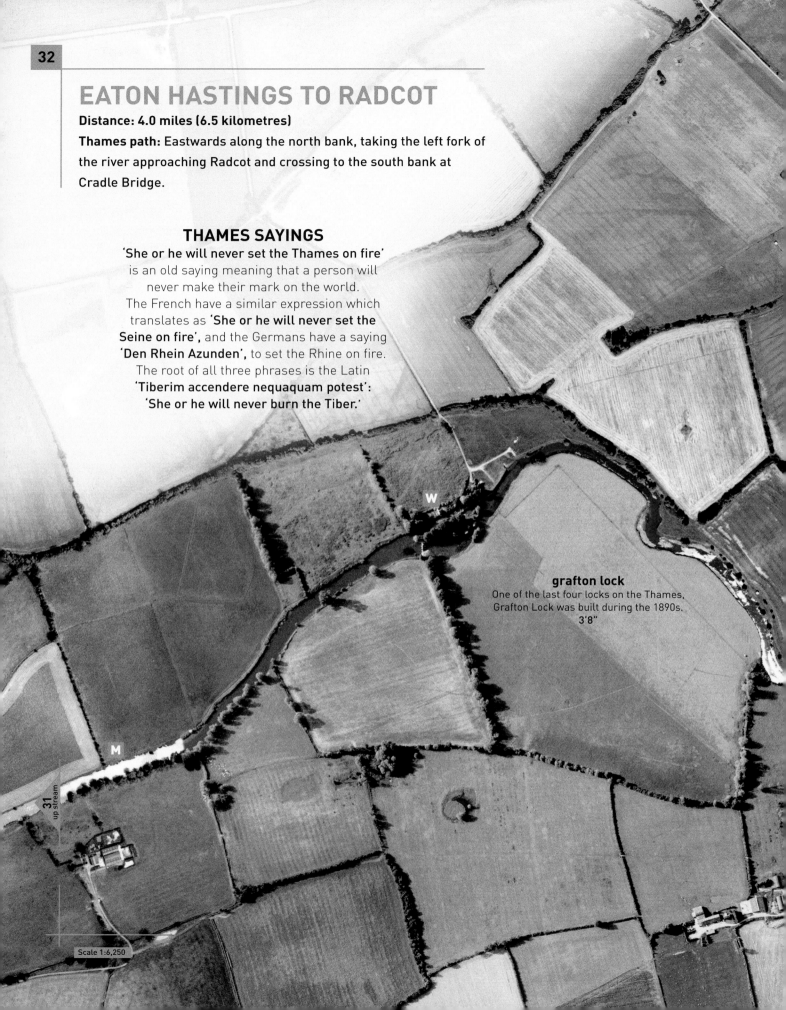

EATON HASTINGS TO RADCOT

Distance: 4.0 miles (6.5 kilometres)

Thames path: Eastwards along the north bank, taking the left fork of the river approaching Radcot and crossing to the south bank at Cradle Bridge.

THAMES SAYINGS

'**She or he will never set the Thames on fire**' is an old saying meaning that a person will never make their mark on the world. The French have a similar expression which translates as '**She or he will never set the Seine on fire**', and the Germans have a saying '**Den Rhein Azunden**', to set the Rhine on fire. The root of all three phrases is the Latin '**Tiberim accendere nequaquam potest**': '**She or he will never burn the Tiber.**'

W

grafton lock
One of the last four locks on the Thames, Grafton Lock was built during the 1890s.
3'8"

M

31
up stream

Scale 1:6,250

34
down stream ▶

M

cradle bridge

M

R A D C O T

swan hotel
The riverside gardens of the
Swan Hotel incorporate a wharf
that was once used to transport
local stone from Taynton Quarry,
which is about ten miles to the
north.

radcot bridge
The oldest surviving bridge on the Thames,
Radcot Bridge avoided demolition because
the river traffic (which demanded ever
greater clearance) was diverted to the
northern channel. The piers of this three-
arch bridge date back to the 12th century,
and possibly stand on the foundations of an
even older, Saxon bridge. The northern
channel is crossed by a single-arch bridge
built in 1787.
11'4"

THAMES QUOTATIONS

Engineer and socialist politician John Burns was elected MP for Battersea in 1896 and later became Britain's first working-class Cabinet Minister. Renowned as a brilliant orator, he was well aware of the historical importance of the Thames to Britain, saying:

'I have seen the Mississippi. That is muddy water. I have seen the St Lawrence. That is crystal water. But the Thames is liquid history.'

radcot lock
One of the last four locks on the Thames, Radcot Lock was built during the 1890s.
4'10"

old man's bridge
This footbridge marks the site of Old Man's Weir, a flash weir that no longer exists.
14'0"

W

M

33
up stream

M

M

RADCOT TO TADPOLE BRIDGE

Distance: 4.0 miles (6.5 kilometres)

Thames path: South bank, over the weir bridge at Rushey Lock and continuing on the north bank, crossing the road at Tadpole Bridge.

Scale 1:12,500

raf bampton castle signals unit

trout inn
One erstwhile landlord had a particularly apt name, and above the door was written: 'The Trout, kept by A Herring.'

tadpole bridge
Late 18th-century single-arch bridge
14'10"

down stream
36

M

S R

rushey lock
The weir at Rushey Lock is a rare surviving example of a 'paddle-and-rymer' or 'flash' weir, though it is no longer used as such. Paddles were placed between heavy posts known as rymers to hold back the water, and when traffic wanted to pass the weir, the paddles and rymers were removed: boats passing downstream shot the weir on the resulting 'flash' of water, while those travelling upstream would wait for the flash to subside before being hauled through the weir.
6'0"

CHIMNEY MEADOW TO HARROWDOWN HILL

Distance: 5.7 miles (9.1 kilometres)

Thames path: North bank through Chimney Meadow Nature Reserve, crossing the bridleway bridge over the Shifford Lock Cut and continuing on the south bank towards Newbridge.

tenfoot bridge

Tenfoot Bridge marks the site of a former flash weir that was removed in 1870 – ten feet is assumed to be the width of passage through the weir. (For an explanation of flash weir see p.35, 'Rushey Lock'.) As with several other erstwhile weirs, the bridge preserves the established right of way that once existed over the weir itself.

12'2"

chimney meadow

Chimney Meadow, one of the largest surviving areas of 'unimproved' grassland in the Thames Valley, is a National Nature Reserve managed by the Berkshire, Buckinghamshire & Oxfordshire Wildlife Trust under the auspices of umbrella organisation English Nature.

CHIMNEY

footbri
12'0

weir and footbridge

35
up stream

Scale 1:12,500

SHIFFORD

shifford church

great brook

W

weir

shifford lock
The last lock to be built on the Thames,
in 1898.
7'4"

shifford lock cut
The Shifford Lock Cut is an artificial cut
made in 1896–97 to ease navigation and
avoid the loop of the river to the south,
which is itself distorted by tortuous
meanders within the meander.

harrowdown hill

duxford ford
It is still possible to cross the river on foot
at this tautologously named ford.

LONGWORTH

HINTON
WALDRIST

37
up stream

thames side farm

THAMES SIDE FARM TO NEWBRIDGE

Distance: 1.9 miles (3.1 kilometres)

Thames path: South bank from the foot of Harrowdown Hill into Newbridge, crossing the ancient bridge and continuing on the north bank.

Scale 1:6,250

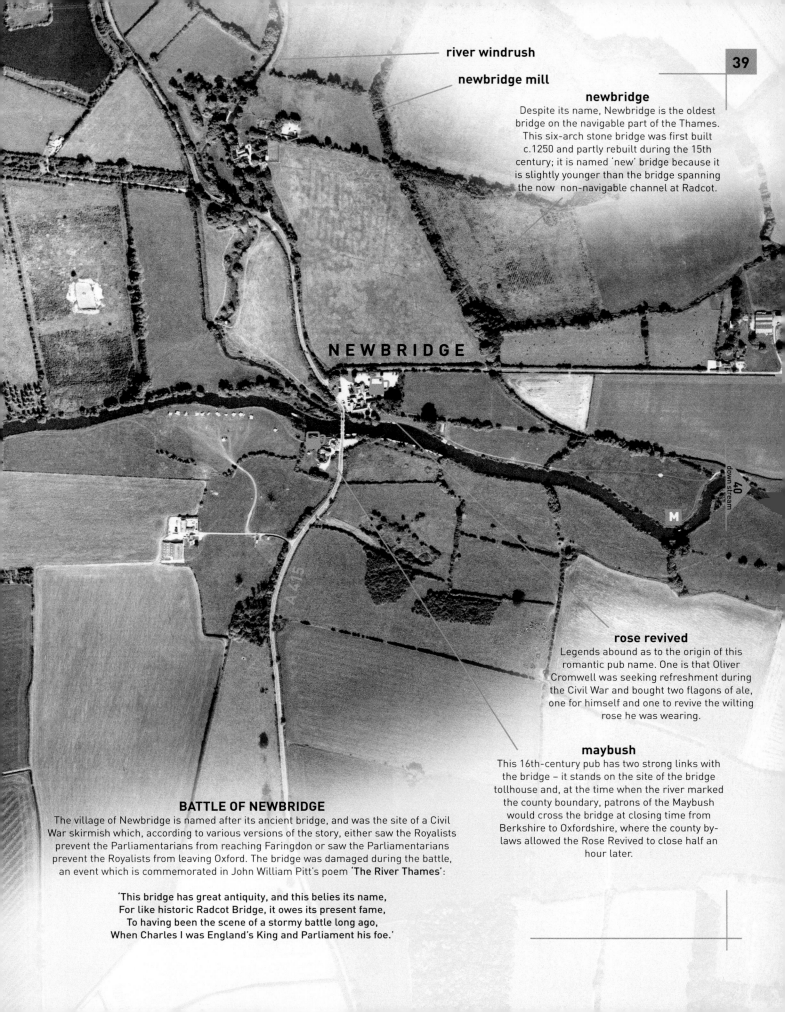

river windrush

newbridge mill

newbridge
Despite its name, Newbridge is the oldest bridge on the navigable part of the Thames. This six-arch stone bridge was first built c.1250 and partly rebuilt during the 15th century; it is named 'new' bridge because it is slightly younger than the bridge spanning the now non-navigable channel at Radcot.

NEWBRIDGE

40 down stream

M

rose revived
Legends abound as to the origin of this romantic pub name. One is that Oliver Cromwell was seeking refreshment during the Civil War and bought two flagons of ale, one for himself and one to revive the wilting rose he was wearing.

maybush
This 16th-century pub has two strong links with the bridge – it stands on the site of the bridge tollhouse and, at the time when the river marked the county boundary, patrons of the Maybush would cross the bridge at closing time from Berkshire to Oxfordshire, where the county by-laws allowed the Rose Revived to close half an hour later.

BATTLE OF NEWBRIDGE
The village of Newbridge is named after its ancient bridge, and was the site of a Civil War skirmish which, according to various versions of the story, either saw the Royalists prevent the Parliamentarians from reaching Faringdon or saw the Parliamentarians prevent the Royalists from leaving Oxford. The bridge was damaged during the battle, an event which is commemorated in John William Pitt's poem '**The River Thames**':

'This bridge has great antiquity, and this belies its name,
For like historic Radcot Bridge, it owes its present fame,
To having been the scene of a stormy battle long ago,
When Charles I was England's King and Parliament his foe.'

A 415

stonehenge farm

THAMES QUOTATIONS
Alexander Pope's **'The Rape of the Lock"** has a section entitled **'A Voyage on the Thames'**:

Not with more glories, in the ethereal plain,
The Sun first rises o'er the purpled main,
Than, issuing forth, the rival of his beams
Launched on the bosom of the silver Thames.
Fair nymphs and well-dressed youths around her shone,
But every eye was fixed on her alone...

But now secure the painted vessel glides,
The sun-beams trembling on the floating tides;
While melting music steals upon the sky,
And softened sounds along the waters die;
Smooth flow the waves, the Zephyrs gently play,
Belinda smiled, and all the world was gay.

39
up stream

hart's weir footbridge
A footbridge built to preserve the right of way that once existed over Hart's Weir.
10'9"

STONEHENGE FARM TO NORTHMOOR LOCK

Distance: 1.6 miles (2.6 kilometres)

Thames path: North bank past Hart's Weir Footbridge towards Northmoor Lock.

appleton lower common

Scale 1:6,250

northmoor lock

THAMES QUOTATIONS

Another poet who waxes lyrical about the Thames is
Edmund Spenser, in his 'Prothalamion':

Calme was the day, and through the trembling ayre
Sweete-breathing Zephyrus did softly play
A gentle spirit, that lightly did delay
Hot Titans beames, which then did glyster fayre;
When I, (whom sullein care,
Through discontent of my long fruitlesse stay
In Princes Court, and expectation vayne
Of idle hopes, which still doe fly away,
Like empty shaddowes, did afflict my brayne)
Walkt forth to ease my payne
Along the shoare of silver streaming Themmes;
Whose rutty Bancke, the which his River hemmes,
Was paynted all with variable flowers,
And all the meades adorn'd with daintie gemmes
Fit to decke maydens bowres,
And crowne their Paramours
Against the Brydale day, which is not long:
Sweete Themmes! runne softly, till I end my Song.

44
down stream

stoneacres lake

caravan park

ferryman inn
A ferry has provided a Thames crossing at
Bablock Hythe for more than 1,000 years,
since AD 904. A vehicle ferry operated until
the 1960s, and a foot ferry has recently been
revived by the landlord close to the
Ferryman Inn. This pub began life as the
Chequers and was later renamed the Ferry
and then, later still, the Ferryman.

red lion
A mid-18th-century pub converted from two
15th-century cottages, the Red Lion is said
to be haunted by a headless apparition.

N O R T H M O O R

northmoor lock
Another ancient paddle-and-rymer lock,
although the paddles at Bablock Hythe are
made of rather more modern fibreglass.
(For explanation of paddle-and-rymer see
Rushey Lock, p35.)
4'1"

NORTHMOOR LOCK TO
BABLOCK HYTHE

Distance: 2.3 miles (3.7 kilometres)
Thames path: North bank to Bablock Hythe, leaving
the river to skirt the caravan park before continuing
northwards along a bridle-path through the fields.

up stream
41

bablock hythe
The caravan site did not disfigure Bablock Hythe in Matthew Arnold's day, when he wrote his poem 'The Scholar-Gipsy':

'Thee at the ferry Oxford riders blithe,
Returning home on summer-nights have met
Crossing the stripling Thames at Bablock Hythe,
Trailing in the cool stream thy fingers wet,
As the punt's rope chops round.'

EATON

eight bells
This pub was originally named The Bells, after the bells worn by the horses working the fields. The name was later changed to the Six Bells, to reflect the peal of bells that had been hung in the local church, and was then changed again to the Eight Bells when the church upgraded its peal.

APPLETON

THE LOVERS OF STANTON HARCOURT

In a letter to Martha Blount dated August 1718, Alexander Pope recounts the story of local lovers, who were struck by lightning and buried together in the churchyard. Pope wrote an epitaph for their monument but Lady Mary Wortley Montagu was not impressed with Pope's supposition that the lovers 'would have lived in everlasting joy and harmony if the lightning had not interrupted their scheme of happiness'. Instead she sent him an alternative epitaph of her own:

'For had they seen the next year's sun,
A beaten wife, and cuckold swain
Had jointly curs'd the marriage chain;
Now they are happy in their doom,
For Pope hath wrote upon their tomb

pope's tower

Pope's Tower is one of the few surviving parts of the 15th-century Stanton Harcourt Manor, built by the Harcourt family. The tower above the chapel is named after Alexander Pope, because it was here, in 1718, that he completed the fifth volume of his translation of Homer's Iliad.

STANTON HARCOURT

caravan park

WHITLEY COPSE TO PINKHILL LOCK

Distance: 2.6 miles (4.3 kilometres)

Thames path: Continuing along the bridle-path to the west of the caravan park, rejoining the Thames at the copse alongside Farmoor Reservoir and crossing the river at Pinkhill Weir.

Scale 1:12,500

up stream
42

F A R M O O R

M

pinkhill lock
3'6"

pinkhill weir

farmoor reservoir
Farmoor Reservoir is the home of a sailing
club and of the Farmoor Fly Fishing Club,
which keeps the reservoir well stocked with
brown and rainbow trout.

M

whitley copse

E Y N S H A M

eynsham lo
2"9"

W S R

M

M

the talbot
The first record of a pub on this site was in 1769, at about the time Swinford Bridge was built. The pub was given its present name in the early 19th century, and is a reference to the local hunt: the Talbot is a hound bred for stag hunting.

swinford bridge
Built for the Earl of Abingdon c.1770, this is one of two surviving toll bridges over the Thames, the other being Whitchurch Bridge (p.94).
14'9"

stroud copse

STROUD COPSE TO YARNTON MEAD

Distance: 3.2 miles (5.2 kilometres)

Thames path: Following the course of the river along the south (east) bank.

Scale 1:12,500

→ up stream
45

yarnton or
west mead

river evenlode
Tributary rising in the Cotswolds

wharf stream **M**

wytham great wood
Seen here is just part of the
600 acres of Wytham Great
Wood, which is owned by
Oxford University.

wytham hill

48

yarnton or west mead

king's weir

M

king's lock
2'6"

weir

47
up stream

hagley pool

M

YARNTON MEAD TO WOLVERCOTE

Distance: 1.5 miles (2.4 kilometres)

Thames path: Following the south bank of the river.

Scale 1:6,250

oxford canal

oxey mead

duke's cut
Cut linking the Thames with the
Oxford Canal via the Wolvercote
mill stream.

49

pixey mead

A34
unk road carrying the Oxford
western bypass

W O L V E R C O TE

wolvercote paper mill
Paper has been made here since the 17th century,
much of it used by Oxford University and its press.

WOLVERCOTE

M

M

A34 oxford bypass bridge
13'6"

trout inn
The inn was first built in 1138 as the hospice for
the Godstow Nunnery which was founded five
years earlier, but it was largely destroyed by the
Parliamentarian Sir Thomas Carfax during the
Civil War and rebuilt during the 17th century. The
Trout Inn was often frequented by Colin Dexter's
fictional detective Inspector Morse.

godstow bridge
The original Godstow Bridge was the scene of a
Civil War skirmish in 1645 but the present two-
arch brick and stone bridge dates from 1792.
8'5"

godstow abbey
The 12th-century walled enclosure and the ruins
of a 16th-century chapel are all that remains of
Godstow Abbey, which was founded here in 1133.

godstow lock
5'2"

Scale 1:6,250

wolvercote common

oxford canal
The canal, which reached Oxford in 1790, connected the Thames with the Midlands, linking with the Grand Union Canal just south of Rugby and with the Coventry and the Ashby Canals just north of Coventry.

port meadow
The meadow was presented to the burgesses of Oxford by William the Conqueror as free common land, and has remained so since.

black jack's hole

binsey church
the churchyard of the the 12th-13th century church at binsey contains a holy well which has associations with legends ancient and modern; traditionally linked to the story of St Frideswide, the well has a more secular literary association as the Treacle Well in Lewis Carroll's 'Alice in Wonderland.'

round hill

LOWER WOLVERCOTE TOWARDS BINSEY

Distance: 2.0 miles (3.2 kilometres)
Thames path: South (west) bank under the A34 bridge and on towards Binsey.

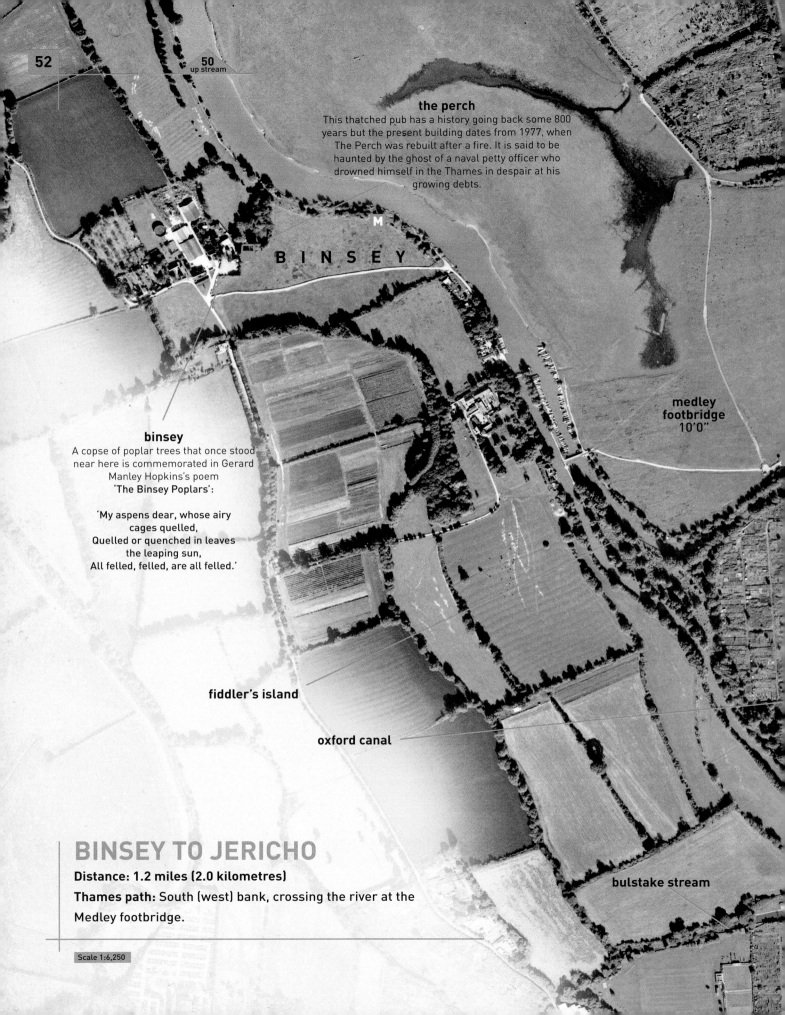

the perch
This thatched pub has a history going back some 800 years but the present building dates from 1977, when The Perch was rebuilt after a fire. It is said to be haunted by the ghost of a naval petty officer who drowned himself in the Thames in despair at his growing debts.

M

B I N S E Y

medley footbridge
10'0"

binsey
A copse of poplar trees that once stood near here is commemorated in Gerard Manley Hopkins's poem
'The Binsey Poplars':

'My aspens dear, whose airy
cages quelled,
Quelled or quenched in leaves
the leaping sun,
All felled, felled, are all felled.'

fiddler's island

oxford canal

BINSEY TO JERICHO

Distance: 1.2 miles (2.0 kilometres)

Thames path: South (west) bank, crossing the river at the Medley footbridge.

bulstake stream

Scale 1:6,250

NORHAM MANOR

WALTON MANOR

JERICHO

OXFORD

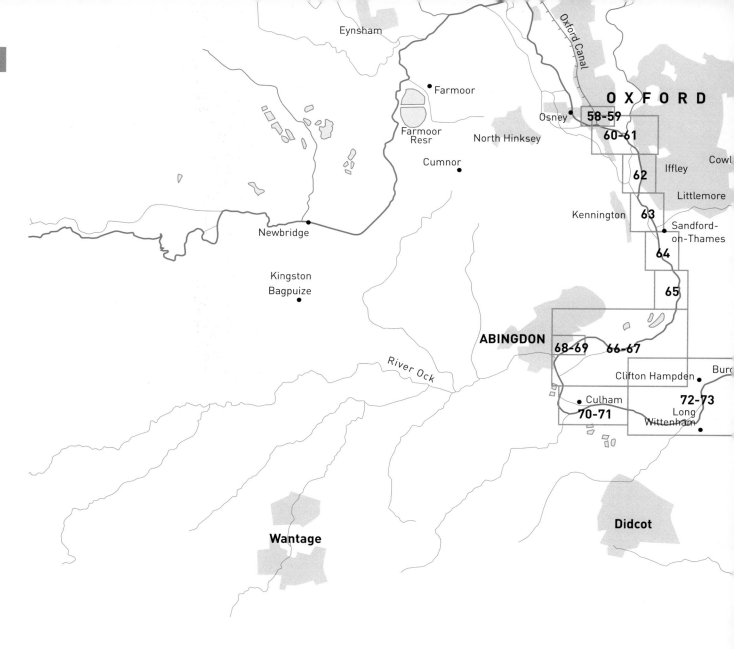

Eynsham

Oxford Canal

Farmoor

Osney **O X F O R D**

58-59

Farmoor
Resr

North Hinksey

60-61

Cowl

62 Iffley

Cumnor

Littlemore

Kennington

63

Sandford-
on-Thames

Newbridge

64

65

Kingston
Bagpuize

ABINGDON

68-69 **66-67**

River Ock

Clifton Hampden Burc

72-73

Culham

70-71 Long
Wittenham

Didcot

Wantage

2 OXFORD TO READING

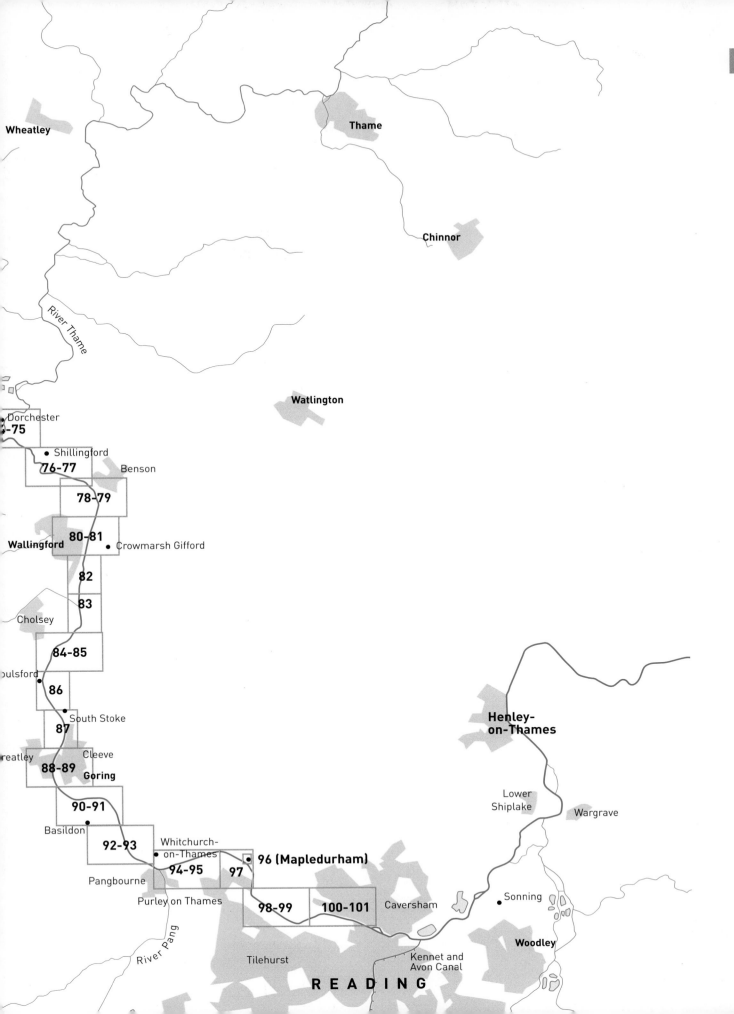

Wheatley

Thame

Chinnor

River Thame

Watlington

Dorchester

-75

● Shillingford

76-77

Benson

78-79

Wallingford

80-81

● Crowmarsh Gifford

82

83

Cholsey

84-85

ulsford ●

86

● South Stoke

87

Henley-
on-Thames

reatley

Cleeve

88-89

Goring

Lower
Shiplake

Wargrave

90-91

● Basildon

92-93

Whitchurch-
on-Thames

96 (Mapledurham)

94-95

97

Pangbourne

Purley on Thames

98-99

100-101

Caversham

Sonning ●

River Pang

Woodley

Tilehurst

Kennet and
Avon Canal

R E A D I N G

52
up stream

oxford canal

folly bridge
Built in 1827, Folly Bridge takes its name from a tower or 'folly' that once stood close by. Another folly, an ornamental Victorian house, now stands on the site of the original tower (**below right**).

osney bridge
Clearance for boats at Osney Bridge is a mere 7ft 6in, which restricts the size of the traffic that can pass upstream of this point.
7'6"

osney island
This river island, bounded by the river and the canal and known locally as 'Frog Island', was first built on after the construction of the railway line in 1852.

waterman's arms
Established during the 1850s when Osney Island was first built on, the Waterman's Arms was extended in 1899 to take advantage of the increase in river traffic after the opening of the power station on the opposite bank.

NEW BOTLEY

head of the river
Built in a Grade II listed former grain warehouse, The Head of the River pub contains the two sculling boats in which Harry Blackstaffe and Alexander McCulloch won gold and silver for Britain at the 1908 London Olympics. 'Head of the River' is a boat-racing term chosen as the name for this relatively new pub by readers of the **Oxford Mail**.

S W

oxford station

M

OSNEY

osney lock

JERICHO TO FOLLY BRIDGE
Distance: 1.6 miles (2.6 kilometres)
Thames path: North (east) bank, crossing the river at Osney Bridge and continuing on the south (west) bank to Folly Bridge.

Scale 1:6,250

osney railway bridge
Just upstream of the bridge is a memorial to Edgar Wilson, who saved the lives of two boys close to this spot on 15th June 1889 but was killed in doing so.
11'8"

foot bridge
12'10"

foot bridge
12'2"

OXFORD

head of the river

folly bridge
10'3"

christ church meadow

down stream
60

The first known settlement here grew up in the 8th century around an Augustinian priory founded by St Frideswide close to the 'ford for oxen' from which the city takes its name. Christ Church College **(1)** now stands on the site of St Frideswide's – the priory was dissolved by Cardinal Wolsey and its buildings and church incorporated into what Wolsey founded as Cardinal College in 1525. The college was re-founded in 1546 after Wolsey's fall from favour and subsequent death, at which time the church was designated a cathedral and the college renamed Christ Church. Close to Magdalen Bridge **(2)** is Oscar Wilde's alma mater Magdalen College **(3)**, famous for the May Day hymn sung from the tower by the college choir;

Magdalen's original buildings date from the late 15th century, while the so-called New Buildings were begun in 1733. Other colleges visible here include: New College **(4)**, founded in 1379 by William of Wykeham, Bishop of Winchester; Queen's College **(5)**, built from 1672-1760 by architects including Christopher Wren and Nicholas Hawksmoor; All Souls College **(6)**, founded in 1438 as a memorial to soldiers killed in battles including Agincourt and Crécy; University College **(7)**, Oxford's oldest, founded in 1249 by William, Archdeacon of Durham; and Merton College **(8)**, founded in 1264 by Walter de Merton (later Bishop of Rochester) in Malden, Surrey – the college moved to Oxford about a decade later, where it

became the model for the collegiate system. The picture also shows the Radcliffe Camera **(9)**, an Italianate rotunda funded by the eminent doctor and MP John Radcliffe and built from 1737-1749 as the Radcliffe Library. It is now the main reading room of the Bodleian Library **(10)**, which was reopened in 1602 by Thomas Bodley, who had spent a vast amount of money restoring and extending the 15th century library of Duke Humphrey –the Bodleian is Britain's second largest library, and is said to contain 80 miles of shelves.

OXFORD

OXFORD

christ church meadow

folly bridge
10'3"

river cherwell
Tributary rising in Northamptonshire

boat houses

56
up stream

G R A N D P O N T

grandpont nature reserve
Created on the site of the Oxford Gasworks

GRANDPONT TO NEW HINKSEY

Distance: 1.2 miles (1.9 kilometres)

Thames path: South bank between the river and Grandpont Nature Reserve.

Scale 1:6,250

N E W   H I N K S E Y

iffley road stadium

This running track is most famous as the scene of Roger Bannister's four minute mile, on 6 May 1954. Bannister wrote afterwards that 'records should be the servants, not the master of the athlete', but he must have realised that this particular record would always be remembered, and the fact that it is still celebrated half a century later is a measure of just what a great achievement it was.

Six runners took part in the four-lap race, with Chris Brasher (later an Olympic gold medallist and instigator of the London Marathon) acting as pacemaker for the first two laps. The time after half a mile was 1 minute 58.3 seconds, which meant that the first sub-four-minute mile was still within reach – just. Brasher dropped back and Chris Chataway took over as pacemaker, completing the third lap in 62.4 seconds, a total time of 3 minutes 0.7 seconds. The last lap would have to be special, and it was. Bannister surged ahead of Chataway and powered up the home straight, breaking the tape in a time of 3 minutes 59.4 seconds. Within weeks, Australian John Landy had beaten this world record time, but no-one could take away the fact that Bannister was the first man to break the four-minute barrier.

donnington bridge
16'6"

iffley meadows
Eighty-two acres of ancient water meadow,
famous for displays of snake's head fritillary
in the spring.

isis tavern
The Isis takes its name from the alternative
name of the Thames (often said to derive
from the Latin 'Tamesis'), and was
converted from a farmhouse into a pub in
1842. There is no vehicular access to the
public – at one time there was no vehicular
access at all, and beer had to be delivered
by ferry from across the river.

weirs mill stream

iffley lock
Iffley Mill once stood close to this lock.
Charles Dickens Jr, writing in 1888, was
clearly unimpressed by the number of
paintings of this picturesque mill: 'It is
hardly necessary to visit Iffley to see the
mill. It has been painted in every kind of
medium, and photographed in every sort of
camera ... Rarely indeed is there an exhibi-
tion of the [Royal] Academy, or the Dudley,
or any of the water-colour societies, without
at least one bit from Iffley.'
2'9"

isis bridge
16'6"

DONNINGTON BRIDGE TO ISIS BRIDGE

**Distance: 0.9 miles
(1.5 kilometres)**

Thames path: Following the
south (west) bank of the river.

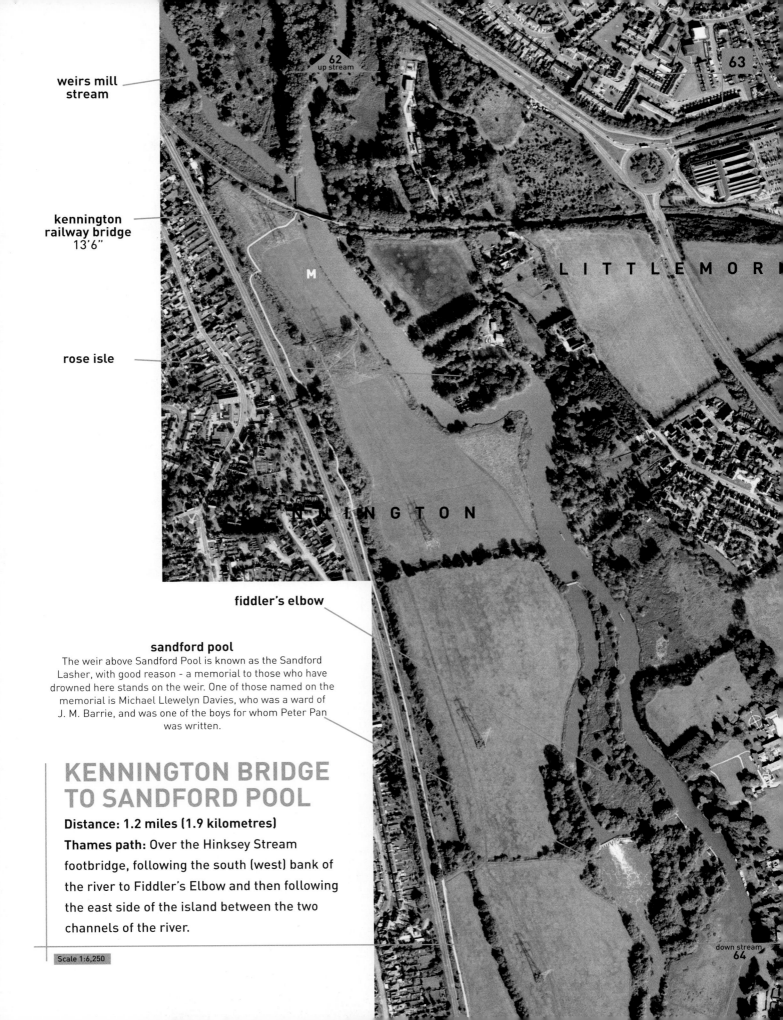

weirs mill
stream

kennington
railway bridge
13'6"

rose isle

M

L I T T L E M O R E

K E N N I N G T O N

fiddler's elbow

sandford pool
The weir above Sandford Pool is known as the Sandford
Lasher, with good reason - a memorial to those who have
drowned here stands on the weir. One of those named on the
memorial is Michael Llewelyn Davies, who was a ward of
J. M. Barrie, and was one of the boys for whom Peter Pan
was written.

KENNINGTON BRIDGE
TO SANDFORD POOL

Distance: 1.2 miles (1.9 kilometres)

Thames path: Over the Hinksey Stream
footbridge, following the south (west) bank of
the river to Fiddler's Elbow and then following
the east side of the island between the two
channels of the river.

Scale 1:6,250

sandford lock
Sandford Lock, with its impressive mill buildings, is the deepest lock on the Thames above Teddington.
8'10"

RAIN AND THE THAMES

The catchment area of the non-tidal part of the Thames covers nearly 10,000 square kilometres, and the average annual rainfall in this area varies between 25 and 29 inches. That means that on average nearly 20,000 litres of rain per day falls in the catchment area – more than 13,500 litres simply evaporates or is taken up by plants and trees, leaving an average of 6,500 million litres per day to enter the river. The Thames from Lechlade (close to the start of the navigable part of the river) to Teddington (the start of the tidal stretch) holds some 20,500 litres when its banks are full.

The earliest recorded flood took place in AD 9, and the heaviest flood on the non-tidal section of the river was in 1894 after one third of the usual annual rainfall for the area fell in just 26 days.

SANDFORD-ON-THAMES

Distance: 1.0 miles (1.6 kilometres)

Thames path: Over a footbridge crossing the western channel to rejoin the towpath on the west bank.

Scale 1:6,250

63
up stream

SANDFORD-ON-THAMES

king's arms

sewage works

radley college boathouse

Radley College was founded in 1847 around the buildings of Radley Hall, which was built more than a century earlier, from 1721–27. The college boat club was well represented at the 2003 Junior World Rowing Championships in Athens, where Radleians Alex Stenning and Oliver Moore won gold medals as part of the British Eight. Three other Radleians won medals with the British 'B' Eight in the **Coupe de la Jeunesse** (the European team championships for junior international B teams), and yet another Radleian represented Britain in the coxless four at the same event. In 1981 a crew of oarsmen from Pangbourne College (p.94), organised a sponsored row for charity from Radley College boathouse to Eton College boathouse near Windsor (p.146).

LOWER RADLEY

LOWER RADLEY

Distance: 1.0 miles (1.6 kilometres)

Thames path: Following the west bank of the river.

NUNEHAM HOUSE TO CULHAM REACH

Distance: 4.2 miles (6.7 kilometres)

Thames path: Following the west bank as it curves round to become the north, crossing the river at Abingdon weir and continuing along the east bank.

66

nuneham railway bridge
15'9"

A B I N G D O N

abingdon lock
6'2"

andersey island

abingdon bridge
13'11"

swift ditch
Also known as Back Water, this was once the main navigation until Abingdon lock was opened.

Scale 1:12,500

down stream
70

culham
reach

nuneham house
The house was built in 1756 for the 1st Lord Harcourt, though it has been
much extended and altered since. The 2nd Lord Harcourt had the village of
Nuneham Courtenay moved in order to allow Capability Brown free rein to
landscape the grounds of Nuneham Park, an act which inspired Oliver
Goldsmith's poem 'The Deserted Village':

'The man of wealth and pride
Takes up a space that many poor supplied;
His seat, where solitary sports are seen,
Indignant spurns the cottage from the green.'

Goldsmith then goes on to write of a widow who was allowed to remain:

'She only left of all the harmless train,
The sad historian of the pensive plain.'

carfax conduit
Built by Otho Nicholson c.1590
as part of the system supplying
water to Oxford, the Carfax
Conduit was moved here in
1786 and now serves as an
ornamental fountain.

lock wood
Flash weirs were often called
'locks', and the wood is named
after a flash weir that once
stood on this part of the river.

science and engineering centre

68

abingdon bridge
13'11"

M

st helen's church

old anchor inn

river ock

Scale 1:3,125

abbey stream

weir
and
foot bridge

S W R

M

abingdon lock
6'2"

abingdon abbey (remains)

abingdon
Abingdon grew up around the Benedictine abbey, which was founded in AD 675 and was dissolved by Henry VIII in 1538 – today, part of the abbey remains houses a recon-struction of an Elizabethan theatre.The magnificent County Hall, built by Christopher Kempster from 1678–82, is a reminder that Abingdon was once the county town of Berkshire before it relinquished that role to Reading (pp.104–105). The boundary changes of 1974 mean that the erstwhile county town is no longer even part of Berkshire, but now finds itself in Oxfordshire.

old anchor inn
The pub moved to this site in 1882, when it was still known as The Anchor.

st helen's church
St Helen's is renowned for its five-aisled nave and the 14th-century painted ceiling in the Lady Chapel. Close by is the pumphouse for the church organ, the last of its kind in England.

abingdon bridge
The original 14-arch bridge at Abingdon was built by the Fraternity of the Holy Cross in 1416-22. The bridge was rebuilt in 1927, when the central arches were replaced with a wider span.

ABINGDON

66
up stream

st paul's church
The church register dates from 1650,
although the building itself was rebuilt in
the 1860s.

the lion
The Lion, formerly known as the
Sow and Pigs, enjoys an idyllic
location on the village green.

culham reach

M

CULHAM

**footbridge
12'5"**

culham cut

sutton pools

weir

**SUTTON
COURTENAY**

Scale 1:6,250

A 415

CULHAM

Distance: 1.9 miles (3.1 kilometres)
Thames path: East bank, following the
Culham Cut (where east bank becomes north)
and on towards Appleford.

GEORGE ORWELL

Buried in the Church of All Saints at Culham is the
author George Orwell. Born Eric Arthur Blair in 1903 in
Bengal, he was educated at Eton College (p. 150), and
then returned to the east where he served in the Indian
Imperial Police in Burma, inspiration for his novel
'**Burmese Days**'. He later wrote about the experience of
being '**Down and Out in Paris and London**' (1933) before
going off to fight in the Spanish Civil War.
During the Second World War Orwell was a
correspondent for the BBC and the **Observer**, and after
the war he wrote perhaps his two greatest novels, the
satire '**Animal Farm**' (1945) and the anti-utopian
'**Nineteen Eighty-Four**', which was written in 1948 (the
title was arrived at by reversing the year '48') and
published the following year. He died in 1950.

culham lock
7'11"

sutton bridge
14'9"

72
down stream

church of all saints
Buried in the churchyard are Herbert Henry
Asquith (Liberal Prime Minister, 1908-16),
and author Eric Blair, better known as
George Orwell.

sutton courtenay
At one time the land belonged to the Abbots of Abingdon, and was
given to Reginald Courtenay by Henry II during the 12th century.

APPLEFORD TO DAY'S LOCK

Distance: 4.2 miles (6.8 kilometres)

Thames path: North bank, over Clifton Hampden Bridge, continuing along the south bank to Day's Lock before crossing the river again to the north bank.

barley mow

The doors of this mid-14th century timber-framed pub are notoriously low, as noted by Jerome K. Jerome in his novel 'Three Men in a Boat' – a sign warns patrons 'Duck or Grouse'. Jerome, who stayed at the pub, wrote that the thatched roof and latticed windows 'give it quite a story-book appearance, while inside it is still more once-upon-a-timeyfied'.

(opposite page)

appleford railway bridge
13'0"

clifton hampden bridge

This six-arched bridge was built in 1864–65 to the designs of Sir George Gilbert Scott, who also designed the St Pancras Station Hotel, the Albert Memorial and the Foreign Office, all in London.
13'5"

pendon museum

A museum containing intricate models of 1930s landscapes, villages and transport, including models of the Vale of the White Horse and the Dartmoor branch of the Great Western Railway.

the plough

Going upstream, this loop of the river is navigable from Clifton Lock to the Plough, which offers free moorings at the end of the pub garden. (below)

church of st michael and all angels

Restored in 1844 by Sir George Gilbert Scott, the architect of Clifton Hampden Bridge .

71
up stream

weir

the plou

Scale 1:12,125

A P P L E F O R D

burcot
Charles Dickens Jr described Burcot succinctly as 'a hamlet of Dorchester of no importance. It receives letters through Abingdon, Dorchester being the nearest money order office and telegraph station'.

the chequers
Attractions at the Chequers include log fires, a grand piano, Granny Mott's steak and kidney pudding, and a Valentine's night chocolate fondue.

BURCOT

LIFTON HAMPDEN

barley mow

clifton lock (and weir)
3'5"

LONG WITTENHAM

day's lock
5'2"

S R

down stream
74

73
up stream

dyke hills
One hundred and fourteen acres of earthworks that once provided a landward defence for a pre-Roman village nestling in the rectangle formed by the Thames, the Thame, and the Dyke Hills.

day's lock
Known as Dorchester or Little Wittenham Lock until the 1820s.
5'2"

weir

S R

M

little wittenham bridge
15'3"

foot bridge

little wittenham woods

Scale 1:6,250

church of st peter & st paul
This Abbey church was built in the mid-12th century on the site of an earlier Saxon cathedral dating from the 7th century, when Dorchester was the cathedral city of Mercia.

DORCHESTER

dorchester bridge

river thame
navigable by very small craft

LITTLE WITTENHAM BRIDGE TOWARDS SHILLINGFORD

Distance: 2.3 miles (3.7 kilometres)

Thames path: West bank and then over the river at Day's Lock, following the north bank and leaving the river at the mile post to join the A4074 into Shillingford.

dorchester
The history of Dorchester dates back to the iron age. Dorchester later became a Roman military station, then a major Saxon settlement, and reached the height of its importance in the 7th century as the seat of the bishops of Wessex and later of Mercia. The bishopric was transferred to Lincoln in 1072, after which Dorchester's status declined, but the church of St Peter & St Paul is a reminder of the town's past importance.

mile post
The towpath changed sides of the river at the Keen Edge Ferry just beyond this mile post, which is why the Thames path leaves the river to join the road at this point.

the kingfisher
Formerly the New Inn

SHILLINGFORD

shillingford bridge
Three-arched stone bridge built c.1830
17'8"

shillingford bridge hotel
Formerly the Swan Inn

SHILLINGFORD TO BENSON

Distance: 2.1 miles (3.3 kilometres)

Thames path: A4074 into Shillingford, turning right at the crossroads by the Kingfisher and following a footpath to rejoin the river at Shillingford Bridge, continuing along the north bank.

Scale 1:6,250

WB YEATS

Irish poet W.B. Yeats stayed in Shillingford with his wife for three months in 1921. Yeats was born in Dublin in 1865. He enrolled at Dublin's Metropolitan School of Art in 1884, and his first published verse appeared in The Dublin University Review the following year. Also in 1885, he helped found the Dublin Hermetic Society to pursue his interest in mysticism and the occult, interests which, together with a passion for Irish mythology, informed much of his poetry. 'The Wanderings of Oisin and Other Poems' (1889) established Yeats as a literary force, and in 1892 he became a founder-member of the Irish Literary Society. In 1899 Yeats helped found the Irish Literary Theatre, which later became the Irish National Theatre, the company that opened the famous Abbey Theatre, Dublin, in 1904. He published 'Michael Robartes and the Dancer' in 1921 and began composing 'Meditations in Time of Civil War' in Shillingford that same year. Yeats was awarded the Nobel Prize for Literature in 1923, published 'The Winding Stair', which is generally regarded to be his best work, in 1933, and died in Italy in 1939. His body was returned to Ireland in 1948.

BENSON

caravan park

M W R

M W

benson lock

benson weir

benson airfield
RAF Benson opened in 1939 under the control of Bomber Command
but was soon transferred to Coastal Command, whose Spitfire and
Mosquito squadrons carried out vital wartime photo reconnaissance
over Europe. As well as RAF aircraft, Benson is now also home to the
Oxford and London University Air Squadrons.

BENSON

Distance: 5 miles (2.5 kilometres)

Thames path: North bank, crossing the river at Benson Lock and
continuing along the south (west) bank.

Scale 1:6,250

crown inn

raf benson

BENSON

PRESTON
CROWMARSH

WALLINGFORD

Distance: 1.0 miles (1.6 kilometres)

Thames path: West bank, leaving the river to pass through the streets of Wallingford.

wallingford

One of the oldest royal boroughs, Wallingford's charter was granted in 1155 by Henry II, whose succession to the throne had been confirmed in 1153 by the so-called Treaty of Wallingford (also known as the Treaty of Winchester and as the Treaty of Westminster). Under the terms of the treaty, the reigning King Stephen agreed to recognise Henry (grandson of Henry I and son of Stephen's rival Matilda) as his heir; Henry succeeded Stephen the following year. The reason that the agreement became known as the Treaty of Wallingford may be because Wallingford and its castle supported Matilda in her battle for the crown, but in fact the negotiations took place at Winchester and the treaty was ratified at Westminster.

wallingford castle

Remains of a Norman castle built by Robert D'Oilly in 1071. The castle was a Royalist stronghold during the Civil War until it succumbed to the Parliamentarians in 1646, after which it was used as a prison. The castle was destroyed in 1652 on the orders of Cromwell.

st peter's church

The church was built in 1769, and features a distinctive open-work spire built in 1777 by Sir Robert Taylor.

W A L L I N G F O R D

cholsey & wallingford railway

Originally opened by the Great Western Railway in 1866, this branch line was closed by British Rail in 1981. Steam trains can often be seen running on the 2½ miles of track that have been preserved by the Cholsey & Wallingford Railway Preservation Society.

howbery park institute of hydrology

Howbery Park was once the home of Jethro Tull, pioneer of mechanised farming and inventor of the seed drill in 1701. He also gave his name to the folk-rock band fronted by flautist and singer Ian Anderson.

wallingford bridge

This 17-arch bridge has medieval origins but was widened on the upstream side in 1809, with the result that the bridge has rounded 19th-century arches upstream and pointed medieval arches on the downstream side.
16'5"

M

A 4074

CROWMARSH GIFFORD

town hall
Built in 1670

st mary's church

st leonard's church

WINTERBROOK

**Distance: 0.9 miles
(1.5 kilometres)**

Thames path: Following the
west bank.

international agricultural
information centre

wallingford bypass bridge
16'9"

church of st john the baptist

carmel college

THE VANISHING LOCK
In 1838, a lock was built just below
Wallingford at Chalmer (or Chalmore)
Hole but the fall was so slight that the
lock was found to be unnecessary as a
result of which it was removed in 1883,
much to the confusion of Jerome K.
Jerome, who wrote of it in 'Three Men in
a Boat':

'I recollected the lock myself. I had been
through it twice. Where were we? What
had happened to us? I began to think it
must all be a dream.'

Scale 1:6,250

WINTERBROOK

81
up stream

MONGEWELL

down stream
83

NORTH STOKE

**Distance: 0.9 miles
(1.5 kilometres)**

Thames path: Following the west bank.

SWAN UPPING

Swan Upping is a tradition that dates back more than 600 years, and originated in the 'taking up' of swans from the water in order to make marks of ownership on their beaks. At one time swans were considered a culinary delicacy and were therefore highly valuable – but only the Crown was actually allowed to own swans. When the monarchy extended this privilege to two of London's City Livery Companies, the Company of Vintners and the Company of Dyers, it became necessary to identify the swans belonging to each organisation, and the annual tradition of Swan Upping began. The Vintners' Company marked its swans with two nicks on the beak and the Dyers' with one, while swans belonging to the Crown initially went unmarked but later had five nicks: three lengthwise and two crosswise. In modern times, Swan Upping is a colourful pageant which also helps with conservation. The event is organised by the Royal Swan Keeper and takes places in the third week of July between Abingdon (p.66, upstream of here), and Sunbury (p.174–175, downstream). The traditional rowing boats of the Crown and the two Livery Companies are accompanied by a flotilla of classic motor launches, and the process involves taking up families of swans to measure them, weigh them, check their health and record the number of cygnets born each year. Instead of nicking their beaks, each swan is marked with an identifying tag on its leg.

mongewell park

golf course

st mary's church

morning star pub

fair mile hospital
Formerly known as the Berkshire
County Lunatic Asylum

A 329

down stream

83
up stream

ISAMBARD KINGDOM BRUNEL

Born in Portsmouth in 1806, Isambard Kingdom Brunel is considered to be one of England's greatest engineers, and many of his projects, including Moulsford Railway Bridge, involved the Thames. His father, Marc Isambard Brunel, was a Frenchman who, during the French Revolution, fled his country for America, where he became Chief Engineer to the city of New York. He returned to Europe in 1799 and settled in England, where Isambard was born. Brunel assisted in his father's greatest achievement, the Thames Tunnel from Rotherhithe to Wapping in London (1825–43), which was the world's first underwater tunnel.

During this time Isambard was making his own name as a railway, maritime and bridge-building engineer. In 1833, he was appointed Engineer to the Great Western Railway, and built the main line from London to Bristol, including all the tunnels, cuttings, bridges and viaducts on the line (Moulsford among them), as well as the GWR's London terminus, Paddington Station. Brunel built the Hungerford Suspension Bridge over the Thames at Charing Cross, London, from 1841–45 and later used the suspension chains from the Hungerford Bridge in the Clifton Suspension Bridge, Bristol, which he designed in 1829 and which was finally completed in 1864, five years after his death. He is also renowned for his steamships, '**Great Western**' (1838, the first built to cross the Atlantic), '**Great Britain**' (1845, the first ocean-going steamer to use a propeller rather than paddles) and '**Great Eastern**', which was built on the Thames at Millwall, launched in 1858 and remained the world's largest vessel until 1899.

site of littlestoke ferry

The towpath changed sides of the river at the Littlestoke (or Little Stoke) Ferry, which is why the Thames path leaves the river here to join the A329.

littlestoke manor farm

moulsford railway bridge

Designed by Isambard Kingdom Brunel for the Great Western Railway, attitudes to Moulsford Railway Bridge have mellowed over the years. In the late 19th century, within 50 years of being built, it was described as 'one of the ugliest [bridges] over the Thames ... without any pretence to beauty or embellishment' but just over a century later it had become 'Brunel's lovely skewed brick-arched railway bridge'. The river islands immediately upstream of the bridge are said to be haunted.
21'8"

NORTH STOKE TO MOULSFORD RAILWAY BRIDGE

Distance: 1.3 miles (2.1 kilometres)

Thames path: West bank, leaving the river at the site of the former Littlestoke Ferry to follow the A329.

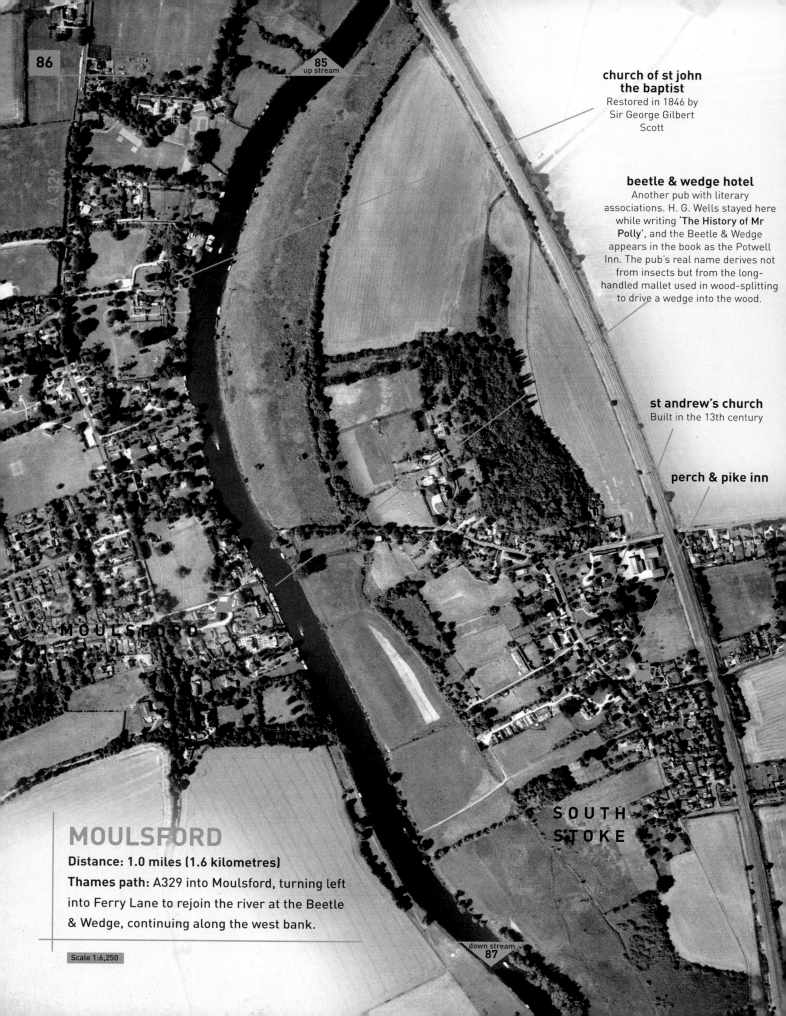

85
up stream

**church of st john
the baptist**
Restored in 1846 by
Sir George Gilbert
Scott

beetle & wedge hotel
Another pub with literary
associations. H. G. Wells stayed here
while writing 'The History of Mr
Polly', and the Beetle & Wedge
appears in the book as the Potwell
Inn. The pub's real name derives not
from insects but from the long-
handled mallet used in wood-splitting
to drive a wedge into the wood.

st andrew's church
Built in the 13th century

perch & pike inn

A 329

MOULSFORD

SOUTH
STOKE

MOULSFORD

Distance: 1.0 miles (1.6 kilometres)

Thames path: A329 into Moulsford, turning left
into Ferry Lane to rejoin the river at the Beetle
& Wedge, continuing along the west bank.

Scale 1:6,250

down stream
87

runsford hole

leatherne bottle restaurant
The Leatherne Bottle stands near the site of
a well which in Roman times produced
water renowned for its medicinal
properties. It is now a restaurant boasting
an idyllic riverside terrace.

spring farm

cleeve lock
Approaching the lock the valley narrows,
with Lardon Chase rising steeply to the west
behind Streatley
2'3"

W

weirs

C L E E V

RUNSFORD
HOLE TO
CLEEVE LOCK

**Distance: 1.0 miles
(1.6 kilometres)**

Thames path: Following
the west bank.

Scale 1:6,250

goring bridge
This is in fact two bridges
which meet at an island
mid-stream.
16'11"

goring lock
5'10"
& weirs

A 329

lardon chase
Downland and woodland
belonging to the National
Trust.

swan hotel

S T R E A T L E Y

M

A 329

GORING AND STREATLEY

Distance: 1.1 miles (1.7 kilometres)

Thames path: West bank, leaving the river by a pathway passing the
church. Over the river by road, continuing along the east bank.

Scale 1:6,250

CLEEVE

GORING

goring
A settlement developed at Goring because the ancient tracks of the Icknield Way and the Ridgeway converged here to ford the Thames.

church of st thomas à becket
Nineteenth century writer A. S. Krausse described Goring Church as 'a picturesque pile of considerable antiquity'. Thought to have been built in the 12th century during the reign of Henry II, it was enlarged during the reign of King John, and contains one of the oldest church bells in England, dating from 1290.

GORING GAP
This stretch of the Thames flows through a
dramatic river valley carved into the chalk,
with wooded hills rising steeply on each side.

gatehampton railway bridge
Another Great Western Railway bridge built
by Isambard Kingdom Brunel (see p.85).
22'10"

GORING GAP

Distance: 2.0 miles (3.2 kilometres)

Thames path: North bank, leaving the river at Gatehampton Manor
and following a path through the woods, running parallel to the river.

Scale 1:6,250

gatehampton manor
The towpath changed sides of the river at Gatehampton Ferry, which is why the Thames path leaves the river to take up a parallel course through Lower Hartslock Wood and Hartslock Wood.

church farm
The 13th-century church contains a monument to Sir Francis Sykes by renowned sculptor and draughtsman John Flaxman, whose monuments and statues also grace Westminster Abbey and St Paul's Cathedral. Jethro Tull, pioneer of mechanised agriculture, is buried in the churchyard.

lower hartslock wood

hartslock wood

LOWER BASILDON

basildon house

meandown copse

basildon house and park
This Palladian mansion was built from 1776-83 by John Carr for fellow Yorkshireman Francis Sykes, who had made his fortune in India and whose memorial stands in Lower Basildon church (p.91). The house fell into disrepair but was rescued by Lord and Lady Iliffe, who bought the property in 1952 and have since restored it. House and Park now belong to the National Trust, which has taken on the task of restoring the grounds.

LITERARY QUOTATION
'Believe me, my young friend, there is nothing – absolutely nothing – half so much worth doing as simply messing about in boats.'

From 'The Wind in the Willows' by Kenneth Grahame, who lived in Pangbourne and loved sculling on this stretch of the river.

BASILDON PARK

Distance: 1.1 miles (1.8 kilometres)

Thames path: Up the hill from Hartslock Wood, passing Coombe Park farm towards the B471 (out of picture) into Whitchurch (p.94).

Scale 1:6,250

beale park wildlife park
The wildlife trust specialises in providing a
habitat for birds, notably peacocks, and also
houses a collection of statuary amassed by
the eponymous Gilbert Beale.

coombe park farm

coombe park

greyhound
Converted from three cottages, the Greyhound became a pub in 1830, although ale was being served here long before that – one of the cottages belonged to the local ferryman, whose wife would brew beer for him to sell to those using the ferry.

WHITCHURCH-ON-THAMES

st mary's church

whitchurch mill

whitchurch lock
3'4"

93
up stream

weir

pangbourne meadow
Seven acres recently acquired by the National Trust

whitchurch bridge
13'7"

PANGBOURNE

pangbourne college boathouse

the swan
Yet another Thames pub with literary associations, the Swan is where Jerome K. Jerome and his companions abandoned their boat on the return journey to London and took the train from Pangbourne instead. Kenneth Grahame is also said to have frequented the Swan while writing 'The Wind in the Willows'.

church of st james the less
The church was rebuilt in 1865 but the red brick tower dates from 1718. Kenneth Grahame, the author of 'The Wind in the Willows', lived in the adjacent Church Cottage.

whitchurch bridge
Built during the 1880s, this is one of two
remaining toll bridges over the river, the
other being Swinford Bridge (p.46).

pangbourne
An imaginary housing estate on the edge of
Pangbourne is the setting for J. G. Ballard's
novel 'Running Wild'.

PANGBOURNE
Distance: 1.7 miles (2.7 kilometres)
Thames path: B471 into Whitchurch, following the
footpath through the churchyard and over
Whitchurch Bridge, continuing on the south bank.

Scale 1:6,250

R

mapledurham lock
Mapledurham Lock dates from 1777, although the weir itself is thought to be at least 500 years older. In 1956, Mapledurham was the first Thames lock to be mechanised.

3'4"

mapledurham mill

st margaret's church
The church clock was given to the parish by William IV and bears the initials of Lord Augustus Fitz-Clarence, the king's illegitimate son, who was made vicar of St Margaret's in 1829. Lord Augustus's predecessor did not want to leave St Margaret's, and had to be persuaded by promoting him to bishop.

mapledurham house
The house is still owned by descendants of the Blount family, which bought the manor in 1390 and built Mapledurham House in 1588. There is no bridge connecting this time-locked village with the modern houses of Purley across the river, and much of Mapledurham appears as it must have done when Alexander Pope visited the Blount sisters here at the beginning of the 18th century. More recently, John Galsworthy set parts of his 'Forsyte Saga' here, and Mapledurham has made film and television appearances in, among other things, 'The Eagle Has Landed' and 'Inspector Morse'.

MAPLEDURHAM

Scale 1:1,625

95
up stream

mapledurham
see opposite

hardwick house
(to the north of the picture)
A Tudor mansion restored in the 17th century, Hardwick House is thought to have been the inspiration (with Mapledurham House) for Kenneth Grahame's Toad Hall. Charles Dickens Jr points out that Charles I often visited Hardwick House to play bowls, and says that:

'if the royal martyr had been as judicious in all matters as he undoubtedly was when he selected Hardwick for a playground, the course of English history might have been considerably changed'.

P U R L E Y - O N - T H A M E S

PURLEY-ON-THAMES

Distance: 1.6 miles (2.7 kilometres)
Thames path: South bank, leaving the river at Mapledurham Lock and following Mapledurham Drive.

Scale 1:6,250

down stream
98

98
97
up stream
purley marina
purley park
TILEHURST
Scale 1:6,250

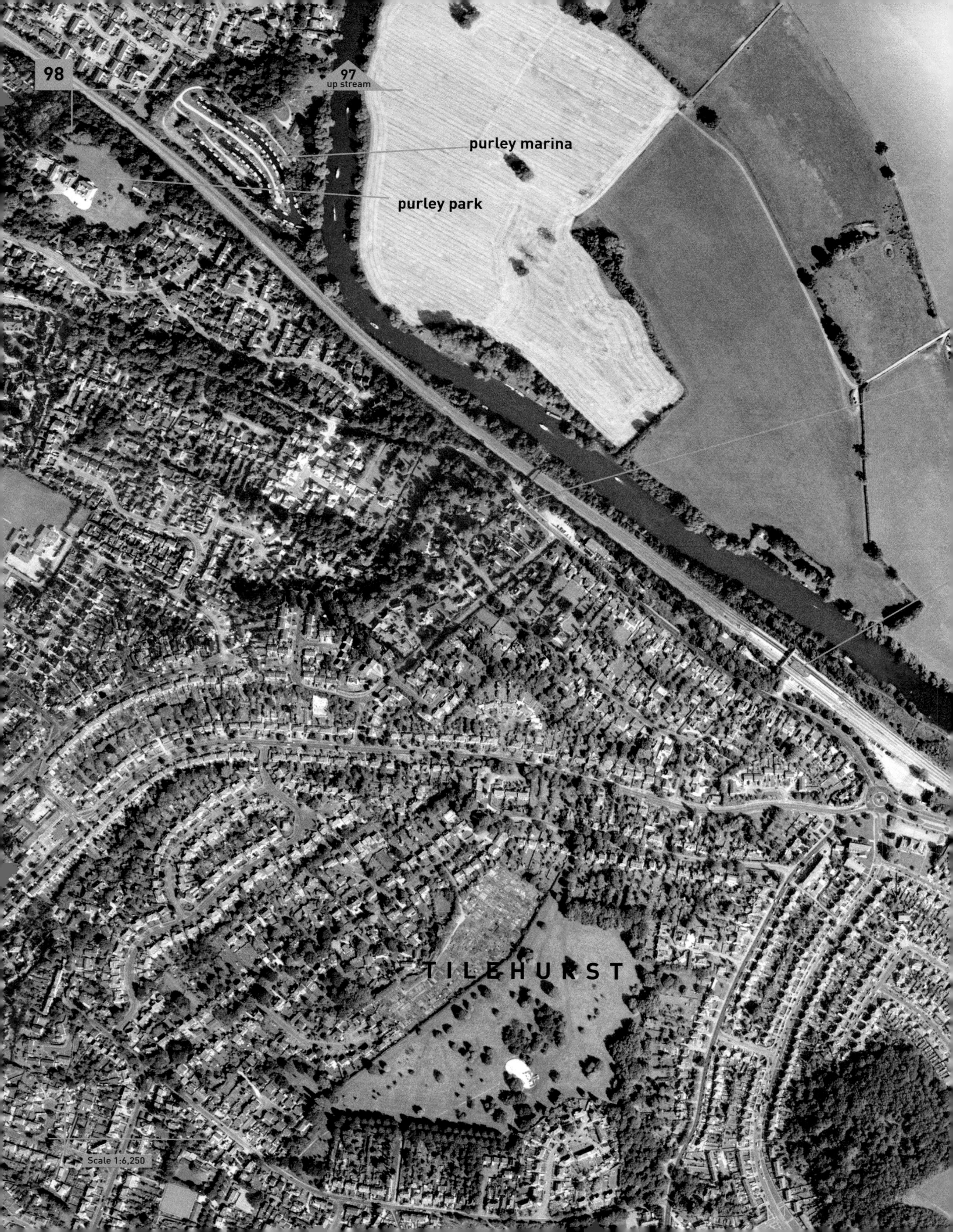

PURLEY MARINA TO APPLETREE EYOT

Distance: 1.8 miles (2.9 kilometres)
Thames path: Round Purley Park, linking with the A329 to rejoin the river at Beethoven's Bistro, continuing along the south bank.

beethoven's bistro
The bistro was previously called the Roebuck Hotel, which gave its name to the erstwhile Roebuck Ferry.

tilehurst station
Late-19th century commentators were able to write that:
'the whole of this part of the Thames is up to the present still in a state of natural beauty, and the little station of Tilehurst, the only building in sight'.
How things change.

poplar island

appletree eyot

purley park
The house (opposite page) was built by James Wyatt c. 1800. Born in Staffordshire in 1746, Wyatt made his name with his neoclassical design for the Pantheon in London's Regent Street, which was completed in 1772. As well as Purley Park, other country houses designed by Wyatt include Heaton House, Castle Coole, Dodington House and Ashridge; perhaps his most famous is Fonthill Abbey in Wiltshire, a Gothic Revival house built for writer and art collector William Beckford. In 1796 Wyatt was appointed Surveyor to the Board of Works, and carried out 'restorations' of cathedrals including Durham, Hereford, Lichfield and Salisbury – but Wyatt was more interested in rebuilding than restoring, and earned himself the nickname Wyatt the Destroyer.

100 downstream

CAVERSHAM

Distance: 1.6 miles (2.6 kilometres)

Thames path: South bank.

caversham

Caversham made an appearance in the 'Guinness Book of Records' after worked flints were dug up here from what had been, some 250,000 years ago, the bed of the Thames – the flints constituted some of the earliest human artefacts in England. 'Cavesha' is mentioned in the Domesday Book as a permanent settlement, and this small Thames-side village has since developed into what is now effectively an up market suburb of Reading. There are no signs marking its borders, something which some locals consider to be either an administrative oversight or part of a conspiracy by Reading Council to subsume Caversham and eradicate any hint that it was once a separate entity.

the chase
(formerly
lower large)

st mary's island

upper large

Scale 1:6,250

AVERSHAM
HEIGHTS

CAVERSHAM

coombe bank

thames side
promenade

leisure centre

st peter's church
Norman church restored in
1857 and 1879

104
down stream

3 READING TO TEDDINGTON

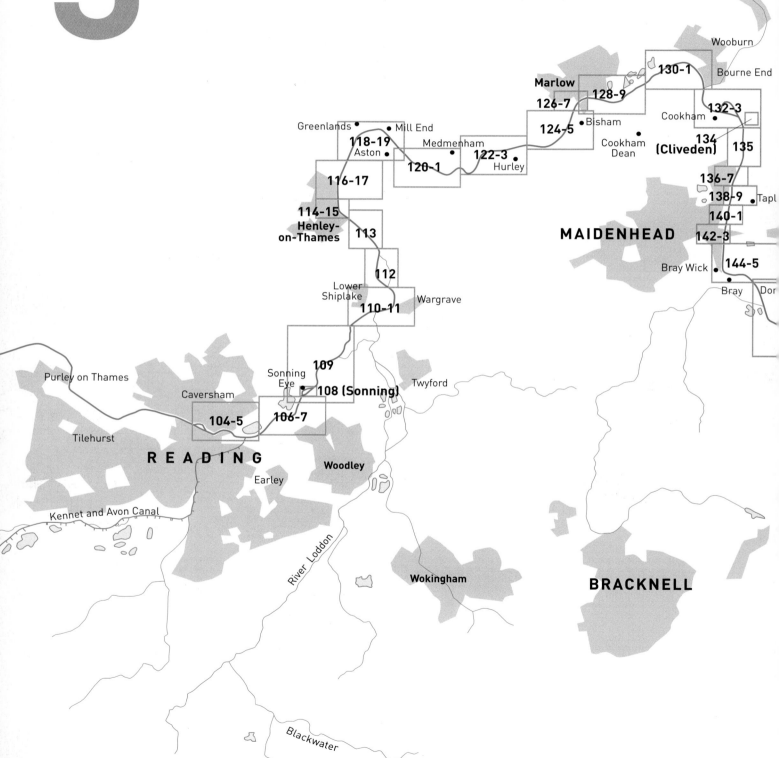

HIGH WYCOMBE

Wooburn

130-1

Bourne End

Marlow

128-9

Cookham

132-3

126-7

Bisham

Greenlands

Mill End

118-19

Medmenham

124-5

Cookham
Dean

**134
(Cliveden)**

135

Aston

120-1

Hurley

122-3

136-7

116-17

MAIDENHEAD

138-9

Tapl

140-1

114-15

**Henley-
on-Thames**

113

142-3

Bray Wick

144-5

112

Lower
Shiplake

Wargrave

Bray

Dor

110-11

Purley on Thames

109

Sonning
Eye

Twyford

Caversham

108 (Sonning)

104-5

106-7

Tilehurst

READING

Woodley

Earley

Kennet and Avon Canal

River Loddon

Wokingham

BRACKNELL

Blackwater

Beaconsfield

Chalfont
St Peter

Gerrards Cross

Misbourne

Stoke
Poges

UXBRIDGE

HARROW

BRENT

HILLINGDON

EALING

LONDON

SLOUGH

Boveney
Clewer
Village

Eton

150-1

148-9

152-3

Datchet

WINDSOR

154-5

Old Windsor

156-7

RICHMOND

158-9 • Wraysbury

HOUNSLOW

KINGSTON
UPON
THAMES

160-1 • Hythe End

Teddington

Egham **162-3** STAINES

164-5

185

Hampton

176-7

178-9

184

Laleham

Sunbury

Virginia
Water

166-7

174-5

East
Molesey

182-3

Surbiton

Sunninghill

unninghill

Sunningdale

168-9

Shepperton

172-3

Thames Ditton

180-1 (Hampton Court)

Chertsey

170-1

Walton-on-Thames

Weybridge

ESHER

Addlestone

Bourne

Mole

Byfleet Wey

Oxshott

101
up stream

4

1

6

5

3

W

M

L O W E R

weir

7

caversham lock
4'9"

reading central station

Scale 1:6,250

caversham bridge (1)

The original Caversham Bridge was a wooden structure built in 1231 with a chapel dedicated to St Anne on what is now Piper's Island. The first bridge was replaced in 1869 by a latticed iron bridge, and the current twin-span concrete bridge was opened in 1926 by Edward, Prince of Wales, later (briefly) Edward VIII.
15'0"

READING

Distance: 1.8 miles (2.9 kilometres)
Thames path: South bank, under Caversham Bridge, then over the Horseshoe Bridge across the River Kennet, continuing on the south bank.

river kennet (2)

Tributary which rises near Silbury Hill and became part of the Kennet & Avon Canal when the Rivers Kennet and Avon were linked to form a navigation from here to the Bristol Channel. The canal was opened in 1810.

fry's island (3)

Also known as de Montfort Island, Fry's Island was the scene of a duel in 1163 between two of Henry II's knights, Robert de Montfort and Henry de Essex – de Montfort won, hence the alternative name of the island

the griffin (4)

This pub, dating from 1911, stands on the site of a 17th-century inn and takes its name from the coat of arms of Lord Craven, who was Lord of the Manor of Caversham when the original inn was built.

piper's island bar (5)

Supposedly named after a fisherman named Piper who lived here, this river island makes an ideal location for a pub.

Three men in a boat tavern (6)

reading bridge (7)

This 180-foot-span single-arch concrete bridge was built in 1923, the first bridge on this site. At the time it was the longest span of its kind.
17'8"

CAVERSHAM

king's meadow

view island

nature reserve

horseshoe bridge

2

READING TO SONNING

**Distance: 1.6 miles
(2.5 kilometres)**

Thames path: South bank

holme park

Charles Dickens Jr, who was not easily impressed, waxes lyrical about the Thames at Holme Park: 'the river which is here narrowed by islands covered with osiers and pollard willows and shut in at the bend by the noble forest trees of Holme Park, presents the appearance of a placid lake. The contrast of colour between the bright light greens of the foreground trees, the richer tints of the grassy meadow in the middle distance, and the dark, almost sombre masses of the towering chestnuts in the background, form a picture not easily forgotten'.

reading blue coat school

The country house of Holme Park became the home of Reading Blue Coat school in 1947, having been used by the Royal Veterinary College during World War II. The school was founded by Richard Aldworth, who was born in Reading and, in 1646, bequeathed money and property 'to pay for the education and bringing up of twenty poor male children, being the children of honest, religious men of the town of Reading ... to be dieted and clothed similarly to the children in Christ's Hospital in London'.

caversham lakes

**marina
S R W**

up stream
105

sonning lock
(see page 108)

108
down stream

holme park
(reading blue
coat school)

W O O D L E Y

Scale 1:6,250

french horn

sonning bridge
14'2"

great
house

bull inn

1

2

sonning lock
5'4"

R

SONNING

Thames path: South bank, over the river at Sonning Bridge and continuing on the north bank.

Scale 1:6,250

sonning
In the mid-19th century, poet and lockkeeper James Sadler wrote:

'Is there a spot more lovely than the rest,
By art improved, by nature truly blest?
A noble river at its base is running,
It is a little village known as Sonning.'

sonning mill (1)
The 18th century flour mill has been converted into a theatre and restaurant.

sonning bridge
An 11-arch brick bridge spanning the county boundary between Oxfordshire and Berkshire, Sonning Bridge was built c1775 to replace an earlier wooden bridge.
14'2"

st andrew's church (2)
The mainly 19th century church incorporates buttressed walls that were once part of the palace of the Bishops of Salisbury.

the warren

borough
marsh

the lynch

hallsmead ait

st patrick's
stream
(unnavigable)

st patrick's
bridge

C H A R V I L

S O N N I N G

SONNING TO BOROUGH MARSH

Distance: 2.5 miles (4.0 kilometres)

Thames path: North bank.

Scale 1:6,250

SHIPLAKE TO WARGRAVE

Distance: 1.7 miles (2.7 kilometres)

Thames path: North bank, turning north at Shiplake Lock and leaving the river to pass through Lower Shiplake.

L O W E R
S H I P L A K E

church of st peter & st paul
Tennyson married Emily Sellwood here in 1850. The church was restored shortly afterwards, and re-opened in 1870.

shiplake lock 5'4"

S R W

shiplake house

weirs

A-4155

S H I P L A K E

shiplake college

phillimore's island

up stream
109

Scale 1:6,250

lash brook

andrew duncan
house

st george & dragon

shiplake railway bridge
17'10"

wargrave manor

st mary's church
Wargrave Church was burned down in
1914 by the suffragettes, supposedly
because the vicar refused to remove the
word 'obey' from the marriage vows.
The Hannen Mausoleum in the
churchyard is by Lutyens.

W A R G R A V E

A 321

river loddon
The swampy ground where the Loddon joins the Thames is the home
of **Leucojum aestivum**, better known as the Loddon Lily or summer
snowflake. Loddon Pondweed is also native to this area.

ferry eyot
Site of the former Bolney Ferry

hennerton backwater

bolney court

poplar eyot

hardbuck eyot

lashbrook ferry
Site of the former ferry where the towpath changed sides of the river to avoid the garden of just one house. The towpath recrossed the river less than a mile downstream at Bolney Ferry.

baskerville arms

wargrave marsh

WARGRAVE MARSH

Distance: 1.1 miles (1.8 kilometres)

Thames path: Crosses the railway just north of Shiplake Station, skirting Bolney Court to rejoin the river at Poplar Eyot.

Scale 1:6,250

rod eyot

M

happy
valley

marsh lock
4'4"
and weirs

marsh lock
The lock, with its smart Georgian lockhouse, is situated midstream, reached by a wooden causeway at each end.

park place
Once the home of General Conway, who financed the rebuilding of Henley Bridge (p.115 & p.116).

happy valley
The estate road from the river to Park Place runs along this implausibly - named valley.

the druid's temple
A megalithic chambered tomb discovered on the Channel Island of Jersey in 1785 and presented to Marshal Conway, who was governor of the island at the time. When he retired to Park Place, the temple was dismantled, shipped to the Thames Valley by barge, and rebuilt here.

THE DRUID'S TEMPLE TO HENLEY

Distance: 1.1 miles (1.8 kilometres)
Thames path: South bank, following the lock causeway and continuing along the south bank towards Henley-on-Thames.

Scale 1:6,250

HENLEY-ON-THAMES

Distance: 0.6 miles (0.9 kilometres)

Thames path: West bank through Mill Meadows, crossing Henley Bridge and continuing on the east bank along the regatta course.

henley-on-thames

Henley is a market town described by Charles Dickens' son in 1888 as 'the Mecca of the rowing man and one of the most favourite places of pilgrimage for anglers'. Dickens goes on to say that 'it is as good a place to stay at for the tourist who takes no interest in oars or rods, punts or wager-boats, as can well be desired'.

red lion hotel (1)

Fifteenth-century hotel visited by King Charles I, the writer Samuel Johnson together with his biographer James Boswell, and the poet William Shenstone, who is said to have scratched the following verse on a window-pane at the hotel:

'Whoe'er has travelled life's dull round,
Where'er his stages may have been,
May sigh to think that he has found
The warmest welcome, at an inn.'

st mary's church (2)

The 16th-century church tower is a prominent and oft-photographed landmark. Restored in 1853, the church contains monuments to Lady Elizabeth Periam, General Dumouriez and Richard Jennings, a master builder of St Paul's Cathedral.

henley bridge (3)

The present five-arch stone bridge was designed by William Hayward in 1781 and completed in 1786 after his death. It replaced a wooden bridge that was damaged in the Civil War, declared unsafe in 1754 and destroyed by a flood in 1774 – a ferry operated between 1754 and the completion of Hayward's bridge. The keystones of the centre arch are adorned with two stone masks sculpted by Mrs Damer, daughter of General Conway (who financed the bridge) and a cousin of Horace Walpole: a mask of Isis faces upstream, while Old Father Thames looks downstream.
14'3"

angel on the bridge (4)

Originally the Angel Hotel, this picturesque pub takes its popular name from its prominent position by the bridge. It is renowned for its fine food, serving fish and meat fresh from Billingsgate and Smithfield markets.

hobbs & sons mooring (5)

Founded in 1870, Hobbs & Sons proudly proclaim the company to be 'Waterman to HM the Queen'.

river & rowing museum (6)

The museum has exhibits covering the River Thames from the source to the sea, and rowing from ancient Greece to the modern Olympics – including, of course, the Henley Royal Regatta.

116
down stream

1

2

3

4

M

5

M

113
up stream

6

HENLEY REACH

Distance: 1.0 miles (1.6 kilometres)

Thames path: East bank along the regatta course.

phyllis court

stewards'
enclosure

henley bridge

HENLEY-ON-THAMES

Scale 1:6,250

henley reach
Part of the regatta course

ROWING AT HENLEY
The first Oxford v Cambridge University Boat Race was rowed on a course between Hambleden (p.119) and Henley in 1829; Oxford won. It was not rowed again until 1836, when the venue moved to London. The first Henley regatta took place in 1839 as part of a local fête; the first Grand Challenge Cup (for eights) was rowed that same year, and the first Diamond Sculls in 1844. In 1851 the regatta was attended by Prince Albert, who became its patron and bestowed the royal title. The present course is 1 mile 450 yards long (2,221 m), rowed upstream from Temple Island (p.118) to the Stewards' Enclosure.

remenham wood

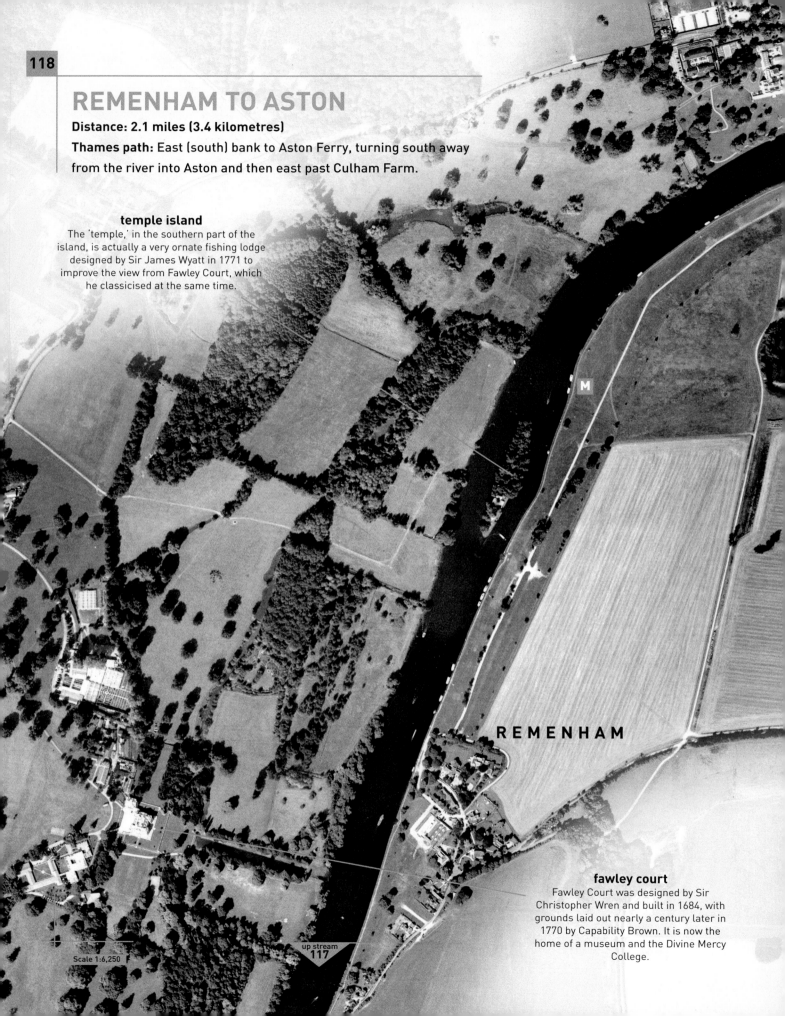

REMENHAM TO ASTON

Distance: 2.1 miles (3.4 kilometres)

Thames path: East (south) bank to Aston Ferry, turning south away from the river into Aston and then east past Culham Farm.

temple island

The 'temple,' in the southern part of the island, is actually a very ornate fishing lodge designed by Sir James Wyatt in 1771 to improve the view from Fawley Court, which he classicised at the same time.

M

REMENHAM

fawley court

Fawley Court was designed by Sir Christopher Wren and built in 1684, with grounds laid out nearly a century later in 1770 by Capability Brown. It is now the home of a museum and the Divine Mercy College.

Scale 1:6,250

up stream
117

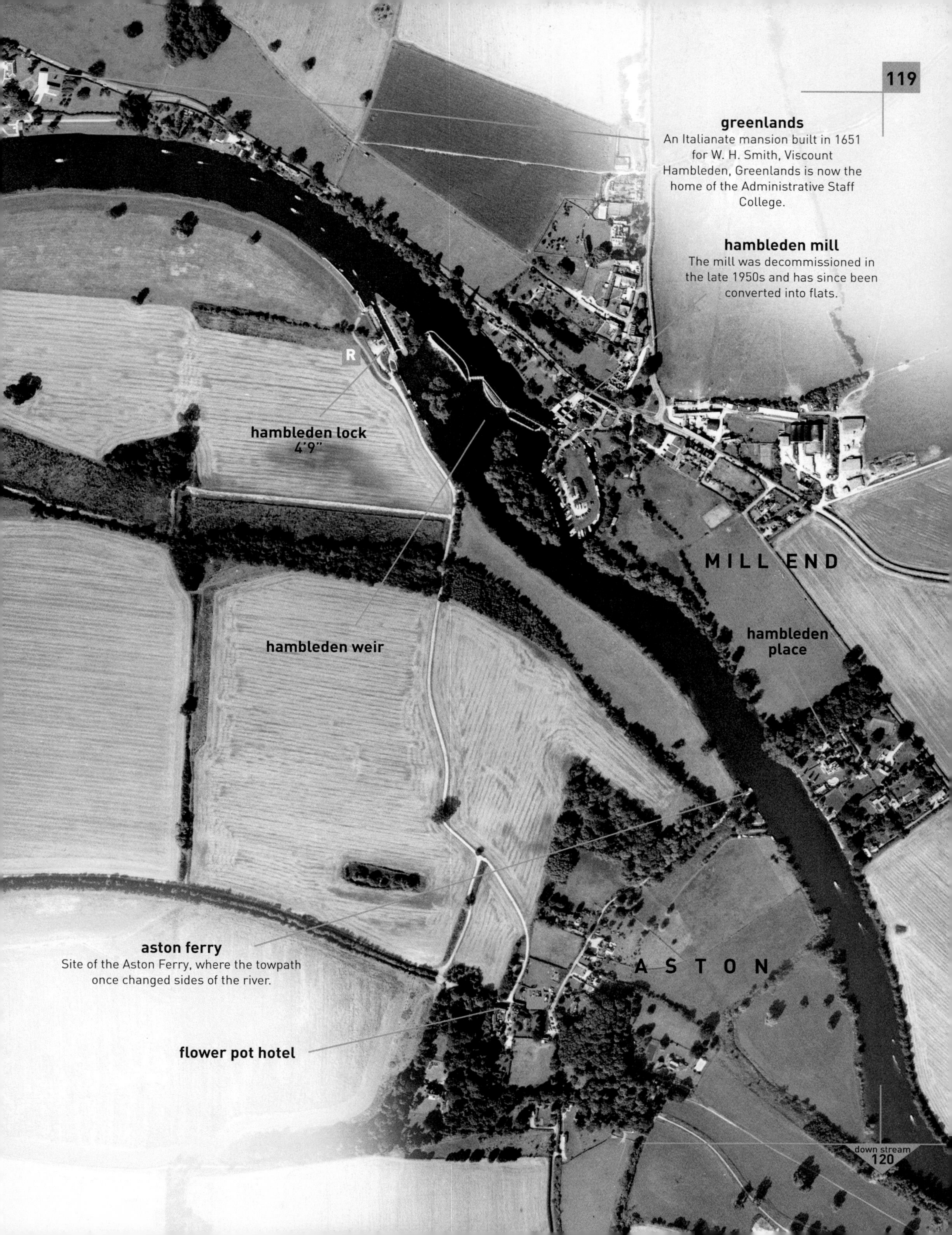
greenlands
An Italianate mansion built in 1651 for W. H. Smith, Viscount Hambleden, Greenlands is now the home of the Administrative Staff College.
hambleden mill
The mill was decommissioned in the late 1950s and has since been converted into flats.
R
hambleden lock
4'9"
MILL END
hambleden weir
hambleden place
aston ferry
Site of the Aston Ferry, where the towpath once changed sides of the river.
ASTON
flower pot hotel
down stream
120

119
up stream

A S T O N

culham farm

culham court

THE MAD MONKS OF MEDMENHAM

As well as being an infamous profligate, Sir Francis Dashwood, whose licentious society the Hellfire Club met at Medmenham Abbey (opposite page) under various names, was also an MP and aristocrat. Born in 1708, Dashwood became an MP in 1741 at the age of 33, and 20 years later was appointed Chancellor of the Exchequer (1761–63), a post in which he served under two Prime Ministers, Thomas Pelham-Holles, Duke of Newcastle (Whig) and John Stuart, Earl of Bute (Tory). He succeeded his uncle as 15th Baron Le Despencer in 1763, and in 1770 he was appointed joint Postmaster-General, a position which he held for 11 years (under Tory Prime Minister Frederick North) until his death in 1781.

Other members of the Hellfire Club included John Wilkes and the 4th Earl of Sandwich. Wilkes, who in his self-penned epitaph described himself as 'a friend of liberty', became an MP in 1757 and had several brushes with the law: he was narrowly acquitted of libel on the grounds of parliamentary privilege, and later fought a duel after being accused in the House of Lords of publishing obscenities. He was then ejected from parliament, fled to France and was imprisoned on his return to England in 1768 – then, just six years later, he was elected Lord Mayor of London. John Montagu, the 4th Earl of Sandwich, was a politician often accused of corruption and ineptitude, whose shortcomings as First Lord of the Admiralty are said to have contributed to British failures in the American Revolution. Montagu was a notorious gambler, and it was his exploits at the gambling table which made his name an internationally recognised word – the story goes that he regularly spent the entire day gambling, refusing to leave the gaming table and calling for his meat to be brought to him between two slices of bread so that he could continue playing while he ate, a snack which soon came to be known as a sandwich.

Scale 1:6,250

ASTON TO MEDMENHAM

Distance: 1.8 miles (2.9 kilometres)

Thames path: South-east out of Aston, passing between Culham Court and the Thames to rejoin the riverbank north of Lower Culham Farm, continuing along the south bank.

M E D M E N H A M

M

water research centre

122 down stream

lower culham farm

medmenham abbey

The 16th-century Abbey of St Mary is more famous for its association with the notorious Sir Francis Dashwood than for its religious purpose. In about 1745, Sir Francis founded a society known variously as 'The Franciscans of Medmenham' (after his own Christian name), 'The Knights of St Francis of Wycombe' (West Wycombe being his family seat) and 'The Mad Monks of Medmenham'. This licentious society rented the abbey as a meeting place and 'restored' it in the Gothic style, with suitably obscene decorations and their motto over the door: 'Fay ce que voudras', meaning 'Do what you like'. The abbey was restored again in 1898 in more restrained style.

HURLEY

Distance: 1.7 miles (2.8 kilometres)

Thames path: South bank, over footbridges on to the lock island and off again, continuing along the south bank.

danesfield
The mansion of Danesfield, now a hotel, is so called because it was built on the site of ancient fortifications built by Danish invaders.

A 4155

weirs

caravan park and camp site

121
up stream

harleyford manor
Built in 1755 for Sir William Clayton,
arleyford Manor is now the clubhouse
for the marina.

caravan park

marina

R S W

124
down stream

footbridge
14'5"

hurley lock
3'5"

benedictine priory (remains)

footbridge
13'1"

church of st mary the virgin
St Mary the Virgin was consecrated in 1086, and was
originally the chapel of the Benedictine priory
among whose remains it stands.

olde bell inn

L E Y

Scale 1:6,250

TEMPLE LOCK TO STONEY WARE

Distance: 1.4 miles (2.2 kilometres)

Thames path: Over Temple footbridge, then following the north bank towards Marlow.

bisham abbey

A Tudor house built by Sir Philip Hoby using materials from the original 12th-century abbey, which became a priory in 1338. For more than 50 years, Bisham Abbey has been one of the UK's National Sports Centres and now provides a training centre for England's football and hockey teams. The Abbey also provides a home for the offices of the Lawn Tennis Association, the British Amateur Weight Lifting Association, the British Judo Association, the English Hockey Association, the Amateur Swimming Association and the British Cycling Federation.

church of all saints

temple footbridge

This 150-foot wooden arch footbridge was opened by the Thames Water Authority in 1989 and provides a river crossing on the site of the Temple ferry, which closed in 1953.

temple island

bisham abbey

temple lock
4'1"

weir

Scale 1:6,250

stoney ware

B I S H A M

fultness wood

THE GHOST OF BISHAM ABBEY
Henry VIII gave Bisham Abbey (opposite page) to Anne of Cleves, after which it passed to the Hoby family, who entertained Elizabeth I here. A room on the ground floor is said to be haunted by the ghost of Lady Hoby, who is reputed to have beaten her son to death for blotting his copybook – the story goes that she is eternally trying to wash her hands in a phantom basin, an idea somewhat reminiscent of Macbeth. A number of inked copybooks were said to have been found in the haunted room when it was refurbished.

inkydown wood

MARLOW

Distance: 0.6 miles (1.0 kilometres)

Thames path: North (west) bank, leaving the river at Marlow Bridge and passing through the town via what is known as Seven Corner Alley to rejoin the north bank opposite Lock Island.

marlow

Marlow is a smart Georgian town with a number of literary associations in addition to the 'Compleat Angler' (opposite page). Novelist Thomas Love Peacock wrote 'Nightmare Abbey' at No 47 West Street, which was at one time known as Peacock's restaurant. The poet Shelley moved into Albion House having recently married his second wife Mary; he wrote 'Revolt to Islam' there, while she prepared 'Frankenstein' for publication. And the poet T. S. Eliot lived in Marlow briefly after the First World War.

marlow bridge (1)

There has been a bridge across the Thames at Marlow for at least 700 years; the present bridge was built from 1831–35 to the designs of William Tierney Clarke, the architect of the earlier Hammersmith Bridge. From 1965–66 this picturesque bridge was refurbished rather than being replaced, which entailed replacing Tierney Clarke's ironwork with steel.
12'8"

compleat angler (2)

Originally known as the Angler's Rest, this famous pub was later renamed after Izaak Walton's book of 1653. Subtitled 'The Contemplative Man's Recreation', the book takes the form of a discussion between Piscator (a fisherman), Auceps (a fowler) and Venator (a hunter) regarding the relative merits of their chosen sports.

marlow lock (3)   marlow weir (4)
7'1"

church of all saints (5)

lock island (6)

up stream
125

128
down stream

MARLOW TO CONEY COPSE

Distance: 1.7 miles (2.7 kilometres)

Thames path: North bank.

quarry wood
Kenneth Grahame lived in Cookham Dean from 1906–10, and Quarry Wood is thought to be the model for the Wild Wood in his book 'The Wind in the Willows'.

M A R L O W

127 up stream

lock island

bypass bridge
19'9"

Scale 1:6,250

coney copse

C O O K H A M
D E A N

KENNETH GRAHAME
Children's author Kenneth Grahame was born in Edinburgh in 1859 and educated at St Edward's, Oxford. He worked for his uncle in Westminster before becoming a clerk at the Bank of England in 1879, where he rose to the post of Secretary of the Bank in 1898. Meanwhile he was writing essays and country tales, including 'Pagan Papers' (1893), 'The Golden Age' (1895) and 'Dream Days' (1898). He retired from the Bank in 1908, the same year that he published his most famous work, 'The Wind in the Willows', which was originally written in the form of letters to his son Alisdair and was later adapted by A. A. Milne into a hugely popular play, 'Toad of Toad Hall'.

CONEY COPSE TO BOURNE END

Distance: 1.5 miles (2.5 kilometres)

Thames path: North bank, crossing at Bourne End railway and footbridge to continue along the south bank.

spade oak ferry cottage
The name of this cottage commemorates the defunct ferry, which stopped operating c. 1920.

spade oak pub
Built in 1887, the Spade Oak was originally known as Ye Ferry Hotel.

spade oak farm

upper thames sailing club

sewage works

129 up stream

Scale 1:6,250

bourne end
This riverside commuter village
is famous for its regatta,
Bourne End Sailing Week

B O U R N E E N D

W R S

**bourne end
marina**

the bounty
This pub began life as a tea-
room before it moved on to
greater things.

cock marsh
Now owned by the National
Trust, the 132 acres of Cock
Marsh have been common
land since 1272.

**bourne end railway
and footbridge**
15′6″

down stream
132

131
up stream

lock cut
The cut was made in 1830

**cookham
bridge**
An iron bridge built
in 1867 to replace
an earlier wooden
structure built
c. 1840
15'2"

weir

holy trinity church
Stanley Spencer's **'Judgement Day'** is set in
the churchyard of Holy Trinity. The church
itself was built in 1140 on the site of an
earlier Saxon building; the tower was
added c. 1500.

cookham moor

bell & dragon inn
Dates from 1417

moor hall

**stanley spencer memorial
gallery**
As well as paintings by Cookham's world-
renowned artist, the gallery, housed in an
old Wesleyan chapel, contains the pram
which Spencer used for transporting his
painting equipment.

C O O K H A M

Scale 1:6,250

BOURNE END TO CLIVEDEN

Distance: 1.6 miles (2.5 kilometres)

Thames path: West (south) bank, leaving the river at Holy Trinity Church and passing through Cookham to rejoin the river at Formosa Place.

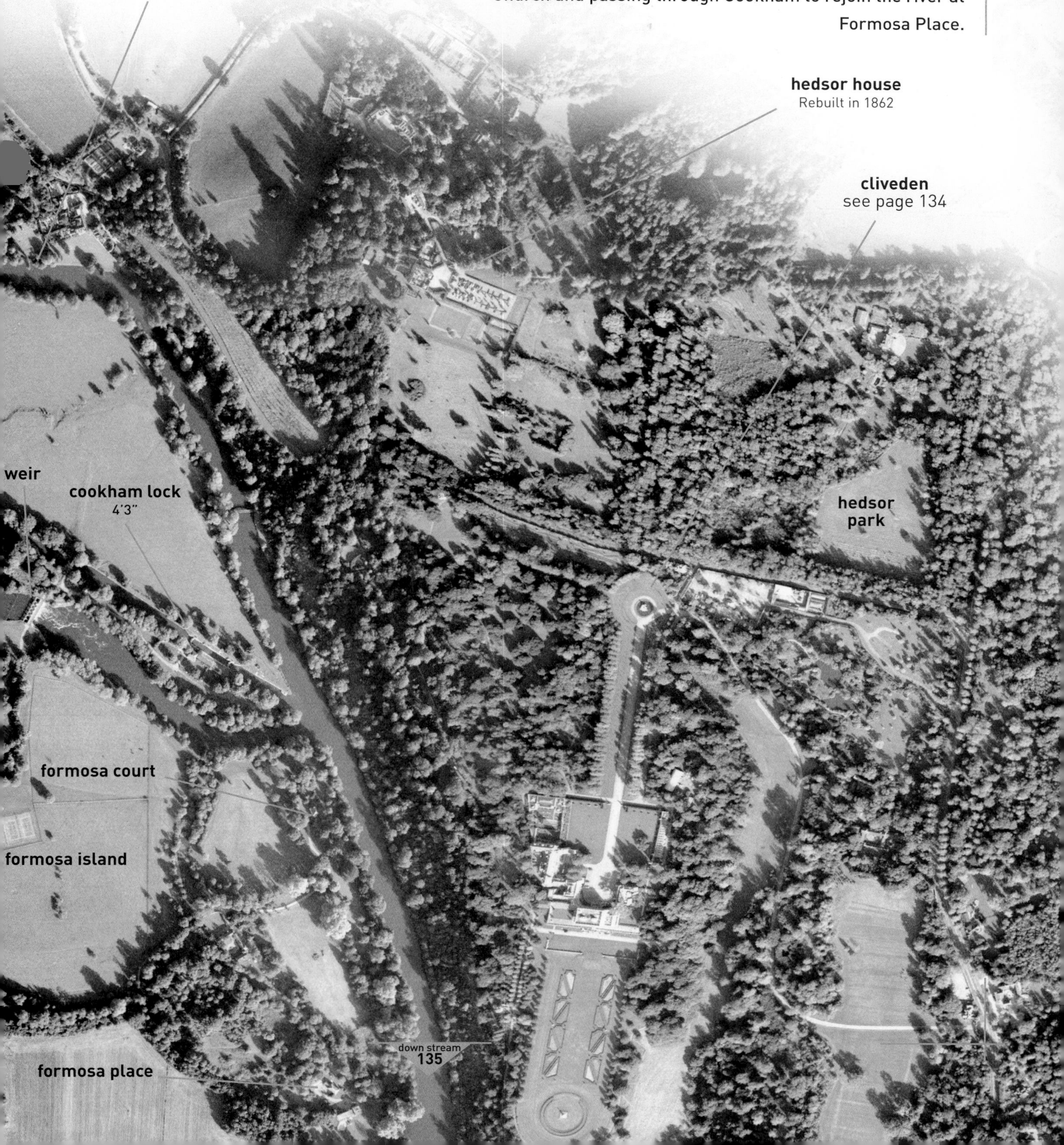

hedsor wharf
Until the early 19th century, Hedsor Wharf was busy with ships transporting timber, coal and paper.

hedsor house
Rebuilt in 1862

cliveden
see page 134

weir

cookham lock
4'3"

hedsor park

formosa court

formosa island

formosa place

CLIVEDEN

The present house at Cliveden was designed for the Duke of Sutherland by Sir Charles Barry, the architect of the Houses of Parliament, and was completed in 1851. William Waldorf Astor bought Cliveden in 1893, and under his ownership it became a meeting place of a group of politicians and celebrities who became known as the 'Cliveden Set'. Lady Nancy Astor (who was the first woman MP to take her seat in the Commons) presided over weekend gatherings of the 'set', whose discussions were said to have had a strong influence over foreign affairs during the 1930s. The 2nd Viscount Astor gave the property to the National Trust in 1943. During the 1960s, Cliveden was again involved with political intrigue when John Profumo made his liaisons dangereuses with Christine Keeler in one of the nearby riverside cottages.

cliveden

site of former my lady ferry

seven gable cottage

cliveden deep

CLIVEDEN TOWARDS MAIDENHEAD

**Distance: 0.9 miles
(1.5 kilometres)
Thames path: West bank.**

M

MAIDENHEAD

Distance: 0.5 miles (0.8 kilometres)

Thames path: West bank.

Scale 1:3,125

Scale 1:3,125

ray mill island
The island takes its name from the Ray Flour Mill, built in 1726, which was converted in 1950 into the Boulter's Lock Hotel.

boulter's lock
Previously known as Ray Mill Lock
footbridge
17'3"

taplow court
Rebuilt in 1851.

T A P L O W

MAIDENHEAD

Distance: 0.5 miles (0.8 kilometres)

Thames path: West bank, crossing Maidenhead Bridge and continuing on the east bank.

maidenhead bridge

A 13-arch stone bridge built by Sir Robert Taylor in 1777 to replace a wooden bridge dating from 1298.

18'7"

paper mills

dunloe lodge

thames riviera hotel

MAIDENHEAD

Distance: 0.5 miles (0.8 kilometres)

Thames path: East bank.

maidenhead

The name 'maidenhead' derives not from the literal 'hymen' but from the Old English **'maegden hyth'**, meaning 'maidens' landing place'. Historians consider that the name arose either because the landing here was easy enough for maidens to negotiate, or that 'Maydenhith' was particularly noted for gatherings of young women.

maidenhead railway bridge

Thought to have been the inspiration for Turner's painting **'Rain, Steam and Speed'** (though that is now disputed), Maidenhead Railway Bridge is a masterpiece of engineering. Built by Isambard Kingdom Brunel between 1838–39 for the Great Western Railway, this bridge has the widest, flattest brick arches in the world: the span is 128 feet and the rise a mere 24 feet.

18'7"

Scale 1:3,125

st michael's church
The vicar of Bray to whom the song of the same name refers was Simon Alwyn, who changed his religion three times in order to remain vicar during the reigns of Henry VIII, Edward VI, the Catholic Mary I, and Elizabeth I. He is now buried in the churchyard.

barge farm

jesus hospital
Around the quadrangle are almshouses for 40 'poor persons'. Jesus Hospital was founded in the 17th century by William Goddard, whose epitaph is carved on a monument in St Michael's Church:

'... I loved not those that stirred up strife
True to my friend and to my wife:
The latter here by me I have;
We had one bed and have one grave
My honesty was such that I
When death came feared not to die.'

Scale 1:6,250

BRAY

Distance: 1.6 miles (2.5 kilometres)
Thames path: East (north) bank.

new thames bridge

Built from 1959–61 and widened from 1969–71, the New Thames Bridge was designed by the engineering firm of Freeman Fox & Partners to carry the M4 over the river. The bridge is constructed of high tensile steel girders with mild steel cross-frames, and has a main span of 270 ft.

25'6"

M4 MOTORWAY

The M4 motorway was built as a high-speed road link between London and South Wales via Bristol. Construction began in the late 1950s, the first part of the motorway to open being the Chiswick Flyover (west London) in 1959. The Maidenhead by-pass, which includes the New Thames Bridge, was built from 1959–61, originally with just two lanes in each direction. The greater part of the M4 was designed for the Ministry of Transport by consulting engineers Sir Alexander Gibb & Partners.

bray lock & weir

Opened in 1845.
4'9"

R

B R A Y

monkey island

The name of the island is a corruption of Monk's Eyot (eyot meaning island). The Monkey Island Hotel now occupies buildings originally constructed in 1744 as a fishing lodge and pavilion for the third Duke of Marlborough.

monkey island

bray marina
W R S

thames field

B R A Y

queen's eyot

bray studios
Film studios housed in the 18th-century
mansion of Down Place, once a meeting-
place of the exclusive Kit Kat Club.
Immediately alongside is the Victorian
mock-Gothic Oakley Court, first built in 1859
and now a hotel.

windsor marina
W R S

MONKEY ISLAND TO
WINDSOR RAILWAY BRIDGE

Distance: 3.6 miles (5.8 kilometres)

Thames path: East (north) bank.

Scale 1:12,500

dorney court
A Grade I listed building dating from c. 1440, Dorney Court has been the home of the Palmer family for nearly 500 years, having passed from father to son through 12 generations since 1510. The house has been open to the public since 1981.

boveney lock & weir
4'10"
W R S

racecourse yacht basin
W R S

windsor racecourse

eton college boathouse

E T O N
W I C K

windsor & eton bypass bridge
20'6"

M

D E D W O R T H

W I N D S O R

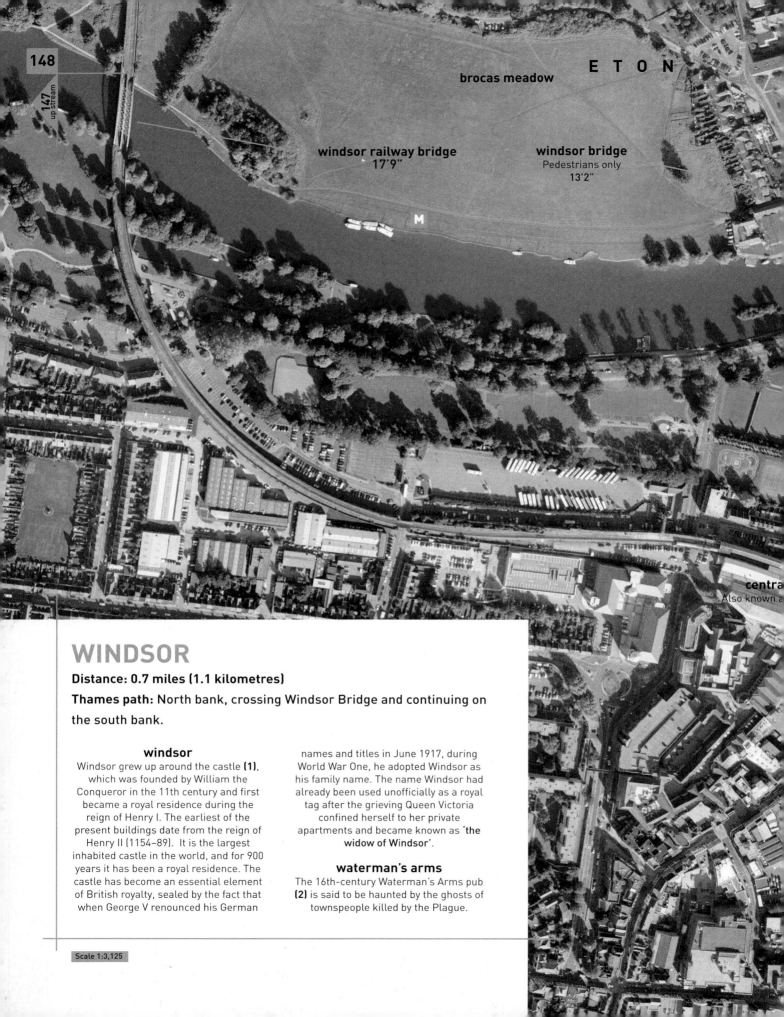

147
up stream

E T O N

brocas meadow

windsor railway bridge
17'9"

windsor bridge
Pedestrians only
13'2"

M

centra
Also known a

WINDSOR

Distance: 0.7 miles (1.1 kilometres)

Thames path: North bank, crossing Windsor Bridge and continuing on the south bank.

windsor

Windsor grew up around the castle **(1)**, which was founded by William the Conqueror in the 11th century and first became a royal residence during the reign of Henry I. The earliest of the present buildings date from the reign of Henry II (1154–89). It is the largest inhabited castle in the world, and for 900 years it has been a royal residence. The castle has become an essential element of British royalty, sealed by the fact that when George V renounced his German names and titles in June 1917, during World War One, he adopted Windsor as his family name. The name Windsor had already been used unofficially as a royal tag after the grieving Queen Victoria confined herself to her private apartments and became known as '**the widow of Windsor**'.

waterman's arms

The 16th-century Waterman's Arms pub **(2)** is said to be haunted by the ghosts of townspeople killed by the Plague.

Scale 1:3,125

windsor & eton
riverside station

2

private
apartments

1

st george's
chapel

round tower

n.

eton college

eton college
playing fields

romney lock
6'7"

Scale 1:6,250

up stream
149

black pott's
railway bridge
19'6"

Distance: 0.9 miles (1.5 kilometres)

Thames path: South bank.

eton college

The college was founded in 1440 by Henry
VI, and some of the present buildings date
from that time. Thomas Gray's
'Ode on a Distant Prospect of Eton College',
written c.1742, laments the
innocence of youth;
'No sense have they of ills to come
Nor cares beyond today'

and contains the famous lines:

'... where ignorance is bliss
'Tis folly to be wise'.

THE ETON BOATING SONG

'Jolly boating weather,
And a hay harvest breeze;
Blade on the feather,
Shade off the trees.
Swing, swing together,
With your bodies between your knees,
Swing, swing together,
With your bodies between your knees.'

home park

This part of the Home Park has been used
for many years for sports including archery,
cricket, rugby and tennis. It is also the
scene of The Royal Windsor Horse Show
annually in mid-May.

152
down stream

151
up stream

victoria bridge

Victoria Bridge and Albert Bridge (p.155) were built during the 1850s to replace a single bridge at Datchet; as well as replacing an unsafe bridge, the siting of the new bridges just happened to create a private riverside park for Queen Victoria. The two bridges, said to have been designed by Prince Albert himself, had identical cast-iron elliptical arches until Albert Bridge was rebuilt in 1928 using concrete, and the Victoria Bridge in 1967 using steel.
20'3"

home park

The Home Park dates from 1698, when William III bought a large tract of land between Windsor and Datchet. His successor Queen Anne had a formal garden laid out in part of the Home Park and it has been much altered by a number of monarchs since, not least Queen Victoria, for whom the Victoria and Albert Bridges were built.

adelaide lodge

DATCHET

Distance: 1.1 miles (1.8 kilometres)

Thames path: West bank, crossing the river at Victoria Bridge and continuing on the east bank.

Scale 1:6,250

WILLIAM AND CAROLINE HERSCHEL

Among the famous former residents of Datchet are astronomers William and Caroline Herschel, a brother and sister both born in Hanover, Germany, in the 18th century. William moved to England in 1755 to further his blossoming career in music but subsequently embarked on an alternative career as an astronomer instead, building his own telescopes and discovering the planet Uranus in 1781 – he originally named the planet 'Georgium Sidus' in honour of George III, who made him his private astronomer the following year. Caroline followed her brother to England in 1772, and in 1787 she was awarded a salary of £50 a year by George III to be William's assistant. Having made numerous important discoveries between them, William was knighted in 1816 and Caroline was awarded the Royal Astronomical Society Gold Medal (1828) and made an honorary member of both the RAS (1835) and the Royal Irish Academy (1838). William's epitaph reads: 'Coelorum perrupit claustra', 'he broke the barriers of the heavens'.

W R S

DATCHET

royal mausoleum
The mausoleum was built during the reign of Queen Victoria, and she is buried here with her beloved Prince Albert.

frogmore house
Frogmore House dates from the 17th century, though it has been much altered and extended since then. In 1792 it was bought by George III for Queen Charlotte, and has provided a royal country residence ever since. The house was a particular favourite of Queen Victoria, King George V and Queen Mary.

FROGMORE

Distance: 0.6 miles (0.9 kilometres)

Thames path: Following the B3021, over Albert Bridge and continuing along the towpath on the west bank.

Scale 1:3,125

royal gardens

albert bridge
Built at the same time as
Victoria Bridge (p.152) to
replace a single bridge at
Datchet. Albert Bridge was
rebuilt in 1928.
18'8"

prince consort's home farm

155
up stream

albert bridge

new cut
The New Cut was made in 1822 thus creating Ham Island, part of which is now a bird sanctuary.

weir

ham bridge
14'3"

O L D   W I N D S O R

308

HAM ISLAND
Distance: 1.3 miles (2.2 kilometres)
Thames path: South (west) bank.

Scale 1:6,250

SUNNYMEADS

ham island

sewage works

weir

M

old windsor lock
Built in 1822, at the same time
as the New Cut.
5'9"

O L D
W I N D S O R

old windsor
Old Windsor stands on the site of a
9th-century village built around a
Saxon palace, but no trace remains
of the village or the palace.

runnymede house
Runnymede House is an 1840s sandstone
Regency villa which has connections with
Tasmania, and is now a museum of the
island's colonial history.

OLD WINDSOR

Distance: 1.2 miles (1.9 kilometres)

Thames path: West (south) bank.

Scale 1:6,250

W R A Y S B U R Y

A TRIBUTARY OF THE RHINE

At the end of the last ice age, c. 8,500 BC, Britain was still connected to continental Europe – the English Channel did not exist, and the present Straits of Dover were a low-lying tract of land between what are now south-east England and northern France. At that time, this part of the Thames (downstream from Marlow) is thought to have followed a slightly more northerly course than it does now. The river flowed across land that was to become the Thames Estuary, joining the Rhine and then flowing northwards across what is now Norfolk into the Rhine Estuary (which extended almost as far north as Scotland) and then into the North Sea. As sea levels rose after the ice age, the North Sea flooded the Rhine Estuary and then the land between Kent and France, creating the Straits of Dover and making Britain an island. And instead of being a tributary of the Rhine, the Thames gained its own estuary where it entered the North Sea.

159
up stream

2

4

1

magna carta
island

brunel
university

3

RUNNYMEDE

Distance: 1.4 miles (2.3 kilometres)
Thames path: West/south bank
through the meadows of
Runnymede towards Staines.

runnymede
Runnymede means 'council meadow',
deriving from the use of these water meadows as a meeting-place – a function they
performed long before King John's famous
meeting with his barons here in 1215 to sign
the Magna Carta. From the late 18th
century, Runnymede was used as a
racecourse for the Egham Races (attended
by George IV and William IV), which were

cancelled in 1886 and subsequently moved
to Kempton Park. Runnymede was given to
the National Trust in 1931 by Lady Fairhaven
in memory of Urban Broughton, 1st Lord
Fairhaven.

cooper's hill slopes (1)
Egham Urban District Council donated 110
acres of woodland on Cooper's Hill Slopes
to the National Trust in 1963.

ankerwycke
This area of parkland was acquired by the National Trust in 1998. It includes the ruins of the 12th-century St Mary's Priory and the Ankerwyke Yew, a tree that is thought to date from the time of Christ.

runnymede pleasure grounds

langham pond and meadow
Designated a Site of Special Scientific Interest, the 'pond' is actually part of an old ox-bow lake that now forms a lowland wetland habitat for wildlife including herons, kingfishers, and dragonflies.

162 down stream

john f. kennedy memorial (2)
Half way up Cooper's Hill Slopes stands a memorial to former US President John F. Kennedy, built on an acre of land granted in perpetuity to the people of the USA. The memorial was designed by Geoffrey Jellicoe and unveiled by Elizabeth II in 1965 in a ceremony attended by Kennedy's widow and children.

commonwealth air forces memorial (3)
An inscription over the entrance to the memorial reads: 'In this cloister are recorded the names of 20,456 airmen who have no known grave. They died for freedom in raid and sortie over the British Isles and the land and seas of northern and western Europe'. The memorial was designed by Sir Edward Maufe and unveiled by Elizabeth II in 1953.

magna carta monument (4)
Commissioned by the American Bar Association and unveiled in 1957, the monument was designed by Sir Edward Maufe in the form of a domed temple. Inside is a column of granite inscribed with the words: 'To commemorate Magna Carta, symbol of Freedom under Law.'

161
up stream

bell weir lock
Opened in 1817.
6'0"

runnymede bridge
Carries the M25 over the Thames.
23'0"

holm

A30

E G H A M

egham
Irish poet Sir John Denham lived in Egham before being discovered working for
Charles I's secret services during the Civil War as a result of which he had to
flee to Holland. After the Restoration he was knighted, and he is buried in Poet's
Corner at Westminster Abbey. Whilst at Egham he wrote the topographical poem
'Cooper's Hill', inspired by the view from the eponymous hill (p.160), which
includes the following lines on the Thames:
'O, could I flow like thee, and make thy stream
My great example as it is my theme,
Though deep, yet clear, though gentle yet not dull,
Strong without rage, without o'erflowing full.'

STAINES

Distance: 1.7 miles (2.8 kilometres)

Thames path: South bank, crossing Staines Bridge and continuing on
the east bank.

Scale 1:6,250

staines bridge
The present bridge was designed by Sir John Rennie and built from 1827–32, when it was opened by William IV.
19'6"

staines railway bridge
21'0"

S T A I N E S

former gravel pits

163
up stream

truss's island
Truss's Island is not really an
island at all, merely the bulge
left by a curve of the river.

weir

flooded gravel pits

Scale 1:6,250

STAINES

Distance: 1.6 miles (2.5 kilometres)
**Thames path: East (north) bank, cutting
across the top of Penton Hook Island.**

staines

The name Staines derives from the Old
English 'stane', meaning stone, and the
name was first recorded in the first half
of the 11th century as the singular
'Stane'. The stone in question is
thought to have been a former
milestone on the Roman road that
passed through the village – later in the
century, by the time of the Domesday
survey, the name had become 'Stanes'
in the plural.

penton hook lock

The neck of Penton Hook Island was
breached by floodwaters so often that
bargemen began using it as a short cut,
leading to the construction of the first lock
here in 1815.
4'0"
marina entrance to the south

penton hook island

W

penton hook

the three horseshoes at laleham
The first record of an inn here was in 1624, since when many famous people have passed through its doors, including Sir Arthur Sullivan (of Gilbert and Sullivan fame) and Edward VII on his visits to the Earl of Lucan at Laleham Abbey.
(opposite page)

thorpe park
Five hundred acres of fun. Thorpe Park claims to be the country's wettest theme park with attractions such as Tidal Wave (Europe's highest water ride), No Way Out (the world's first backwards ride), Logger's Leap, Canada Creek Railway and Thunder River.

marina
Built in flooded gravel pits. Entrance from below Penton Hook Lock.

W R S

fleet lake

manor lake

penton park estate

abbey lake

LALEHAM

Distance: 0.9 miles (1.5 kilometres)

Thames path: East bank.

Scale 1:6,250

penton hook

penton hook island
Managed by the Environment Agency.

L A L E H A M

the three horseshoes at laleham

laleham golf course

M

reservoir

laleham abbey and park
Laleham Abbey, originally known as Laleham House, was built for the Earl of Lucan from 1803–06. When the Lucan family left Laleham, the 70 acres of the Abbey grounds were given for public use and now form Laleham Riverside Park.

CHERTSEY

Distance: 1.4 miles (2.2 kilometres)

Thames path: East (north) bank.

chertsey

Chertsey's local herione is Blanche Heriot – according to legend, her lover was to be executed at curfew so Blanche climbed the church tower and hung on to the clapper of the bell, preventing curfew from being rung until he was reprieved. Her actions were recounted in a play of 1842 by Albert Smith, entitled '**Blanche Heriot or The Chertsey Curfew**'.

abbey chase farm

The name of the farm is a reminder that Chertsey once boasted one of the country's great abbeys, founded in AD 666 and destroyed during the Reformation.

C H E R T S E Y

Scale 1:6,250

gravel pit

M3 motorway bridge
21'4"

weir

dumsey eyot

chertsey lock
4'0"

chertsey bridge
Designed by James Paine and
built from 1780–82.
19'1"

w

169
up stream

king's head
Said to be over 500 years old, and ideally situated in the church square of old Shepperton, the king in question is Charles I – although his head is still attached to his shoulders on the pub sign. Elizabeth Taylor and Richard Burton frequented the King's Head when they were filming at Shepperton Studios (out of picture to the north).

ferry
A ferry service runs, on behalf of the National Trust, so walkers can enjoy the ancient crossing between Shepperton and Weybridge. Notice that, 'droves of sheep will be carried at a fare of one shilling per score (shepherd to clean up afterwards)'.

dumsey eyot

dockett eddy

chertsey meads

hamhaugh island

pharaoh's island

weir

river wey
Rising at rival sources in Hampshire and Sussex, the River Wey was canalised by Sir Richard Weston in the mid-17th century, linking Weybridge with Guildford. The Wey Navigation was presented to the National Trust in 1964 by Harry Stevens. The confluence of the Wey with the Thames is the southernmost point on the course of the Thames.

Scale 1:6,250

W E Y B R I D G E

church of
st nicholas

las palmas
estate

desborough island

footbridge
17'0"

172
down stream

172
down stream

R S

M

d'oyly carte island

shepperton lock
6'8"

old crown
White weather-boarded pub
first licensed in 1729.

desborough cut
Completed in 1935 and named after Lord
Desborough, a former chairman of the
Thames Conservancy. The old course of
the river, north of Desborough Island, is
navigable but may be shallow in places

DUMSEY EYOT TO
DESBOROUGH ISLAND

Distance: 2.1 miles (3.3 kilometres)

Thames path: North bank, crossing via the ferry at Shepperton Lock
and continuing on the south bank. If the ferry is not running: north of
Desborough Island and through Shepperton, crossing to the south
bank via Walton Bridge (p.172).

lower halliford
In 1823, the satirical novelist Thomas Love Peacock bought a house in Lower Halliford for his mother, later buying the adjoining house and converting the two into a single residence where he wrote his 'Memorials of Shelley' and 'Gryll Grange'.

SHEPPERTON

LOWER HALLIFORD

WRS

171 up stream

desborough island

walton bridge
18'3"

thames meadow

WRS

171 up stream

footbridge
17'0"

desborough cut

Scale 1:6,250

M

WALTON-ON-
THAMES

WALTON-ON-THAMES

Distance: 1.7 miles (2.7 kilometres)

Thames path: South (east) bank.

wheatley's ait

sunbury weir
The weir is the site of the original Sunbury
Lock, which has been replaced by the twin
locks further downstream.

the weir
Originally known as the New Inn, this pub
was renamed The Weir in 1875.

golf course

SUNBURY

nurseries

**elmbridge
leisure
centre**

Scale 1:6,250

up stream
173

sunbury court
island

phoenix island

waterworks

R

gas works

sunbury locks
6'2"

footbridge
19'6"

knight reservoir

car boot sale
The Thames at Sunbury provides the
ideal location for that traditional
Sunday morning gathering, the car
boot sale

SUNBURY

Distance: 1.4 miles (2.3 kilometres)
Thames path: South bank.

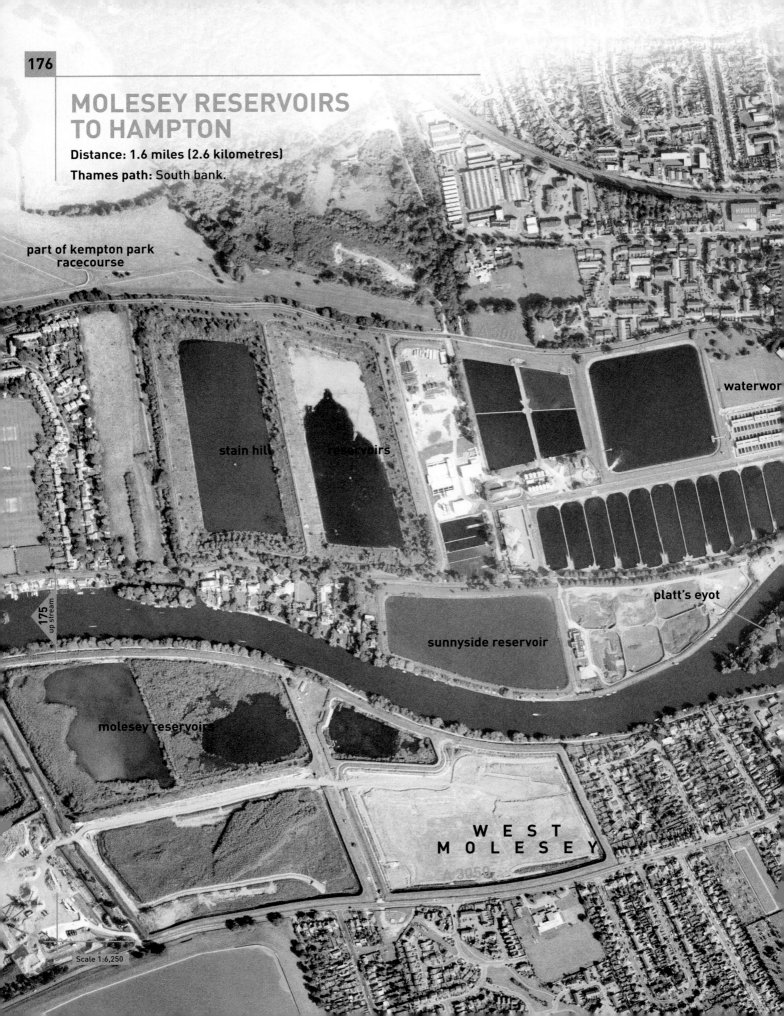

MOLESEY RESERVOIRS TO HAMPTON

Distance: 1.6 miles (2.6 kilometres)

Thames path: South bank.

part of kempton park
racecourse

stain hill

reservoirs

waterwor

175
up stream

platt's eyot

sunnyside reservoir

molesey reservoirs

**W E S T
M O L E S E Y**

Scale 1:6,250

hampton
The name Hampton means 'farmstead on a river bend', and the settlement was recorded in the Domesday Book of 1086 as Hammtone.

H A M P T O N

st mary's church

garrick's ait

178 down stream

garrick temple
Celebrated actor/manager David Garrick bought Hampton House in 1754 and later had the Grade I listed Garrick Temple built in the grounds to house a statue of his idol Shakespeare. The statue was created in 1758 by the French sculptor Louis François Roubiliac and is now in the British Museum; the same year, Roubiliac sculpted a bust of Garrick which is now in the National Portrait Gallery.

hurst park
Hurst Park was once part of Molesey Hurst Racecourse, described as 'a flat oval of about a mile and a half'. A seasonal ferry now runs across to Hampton.

garrick's ait
Named after the actor/manager David Garrick, whose residence, Hampton House, was on the north bank opposite the ait.

tagg's island
Named after wealthy 19th-century boat-builders the Tagg family, Tagg's Island was a popular meeting-place for London society. In the early 20th century, music-hall impresario Fred Karno bought the island and built here The Karsino, which opened in 1913 as the most luxurious hotel-casino of its day. Despite initial success Karno went bankrupt in 1925 and the hotel was demolished in 1972. Current famous residents include Dave Gilmour who made his name as the guitarist for rock giants Pink Floyd.

H A M P T O N

177
up stream

hurst park

footbridge

ash island

weirs

W R

W R

GARRICK'S AIT TO HAMPTON COURT

Distance: 1.4 miles (2.2 kilometres)
Thames path: South bank through Hurst Park and over Hampton Court Bridge, continuing on the north bank past Hampton Court Palace.

molesey lock
6'1"

hampton court bridge
The first bridge at Hampton Court was built from 1750–53, rebuilt in 1778 and replaced in 1865. The present three-arch concrete bridge was built from 1930–33 to the designs of Sir Edwin Lutyens and W.P. Robinson. The concrete was faced with Portland stone and red brick to blend with the architecture of Hampton Court Palace.
19'5"

Scale 1:6,250

E A S T   M O L E S E Y

hampton court maze

The Wilderness includes the world famous maze, which was originally planted for William III as one of four such hedge mazes – plans to restore the other three have not yet been realised. Harris, one of Jerome K. Jerome's 'Three Men in a Boat', managed to get himself lost in this deceptively tricky maze.

diana fountain

The Diana Fountain was created by Sir Christopher Wren in 1713 and incorporates a statue by Francesco Fanelli of Diana, the goddess of hunting.

bushy park

Bushy Park extends to 1,099 acres. Together with Hampton Court Park, it was acquired by Cardinal Wolsey in 1514 from the Knights Hospitaller of St John and passed with Hampton Court Palace to Henry VIII, who enclosed both parks for hunting. Bushy Park was subsequently laid out in a more formal style for William III, including the creation of the famous avenues of chestnut trees.

hampton green

hampton court palace
see pages 180-181

hampton court park

the long water

river ember

down stream
182

HAMPTON COURT PALACE

HAMPTON COURT PALACE
Thomas Wolsey bought the site of the Palace in 1514. A year later he became Cardinal and Lord Chancellor of England, and built himself a residence of such splendour that Henry VIII was prompted to ask why. Wolsey reputedly replied, 'To show how noble a place a subject may offer his sovereign' - prophetic words indeed, because when Wolsey fell from favour Henry took possession of Hampton Court and extended it still further, creating a palace for his own use. The Palace was extensively remodelled from 1689 by Sir Christopher Wren for William III and Queen Mary.

great gatehouse (1)

base court (2)

clock court (3)

fountain court (4)
Designed by Christopher Wren, with the eponymous fountain at its centre

lower orangery (5)

privy garden (6)
Another of William III's creations, the formal Privy Garden includes a wrought iron screen by Jean Tijou

broad walk (7)
Laid out for Henry VIII

fountain garden (8)
The distinctive semicircular garden that fans out from the eastern front of the palace was laid out for William III and at one time featured 13 fountains.

wilderness (9)
Henry VIII's 16th-century tiltyard, laid out as a venue for jousting tournaments, was transformed at the end of the 17th century by William III into this formal evergreen garden known as the Wilderness.

long water (10)
Laid out for Charles II

Scale 1:3,125

179
up stream

hampton court park
The 622-acre Hampton Court Park, which once belonged to the Knights Hospitaller of St John, was acquired by Thomas Wolsey in 1514 and passed with Bushy Park and the Palace buildings to Henry VIII. Much of the southern part of the park visible here is now a golf course.

ditton field

thames ditton island

the pavilion

home park
golf course

ye olde swan
Henry VIII visited this ancient pub, parts of which are said to date back to the 13th century.

W R S

footbridge

T H A M E S
D I T T O N

THAMES DITTON

Distance: 2.0 miles (3.2 kilometres)

Thames path: North bank.

Scale 1:6,250

W R S

W R S

seething wells
This district of Surbiton
was once renowned for its
therapeutic springs.

S U R B I T O N

surbiton
Surbiton was created because Kingston
upon Thames, immediately to the north
(p.184), refused to accept the railway.
Surbiton was initially known as Kingston
New Town or, more sarcastically,
Kingston-on-Railway, but it soon became
quite fashionable and earned itself the
more pleasing nickname 'Queen of the
London Suburbs'.

waterworks
The waterworks were
built in 1852 and are
notable for their
Romanesque towers.

KINGSTON UPON THAMES

Distance: 0.9 miles (1.5 kilometres)

Thames path: West bank, over Kingston Bridge and continuing on the east bank.

kingston upon thames

Kingston upon Thames is the oldest of three Royal Boroughs in England, having gained its first charter from King John in 1200. Kingston's prominence as a market town was assured in 1628 when Charles I granted a charter forbidding any other market from being held within a seven-mile radius.

kingston bridge

There has been a bridge at Kingston at least since medieval times, and the remains of a 12th-century bridge have been incorporated in the John Lewis store adjacent to the present bridge. The latest incarnation of Kingston Bridge was designed by Edward Lapidge and built from 1825–28.
23'11"

guildhall

Kingston upon Thames saw the coronation of no less than seven Saxon kings. The coronation stone stands outside the Guildhall and supposedly marks the place where the Saxon kings were crowned, although doubts have been raised as to the authenticity of the stone.

surrey county hall

kingston university

ferry

raven's ait

185
down stream

W R

up stream
183

HAMPTON WICK

**Distance: 0.9 miles
(1.5 kilometres)**

Thames path: East bank.

trowlock island

steven's eyots

canbury gardens

hampton wick

For many years Hampton (p.177) and
Hampton Wick were part of the same
parish, leading to a number of disputes
which were partially solved by an agreement
of 1698 dividing the parish income
proportionately between the Town and the
Wick. (Wick literally means 'site of an
earlier settlement' but in this case means
'hamlet'.) When Hampton rebuilt its parish
church in 1829–31, Hampton Wick built its
own church and formed the new parish of
St John, thus asserting an independent
identity, though not for long – in 1880
Hampton Wick was described as 'practically
a suburb of Kingston'.

**KINGSTON
UPON
THAMES**

kingston railway bridge

The first railway bridge here was a cast-
iron structure built from 1860–63. It
was replaced in 1907 with a steel bridge
designed by J.W. Jacomb Hood.
22'4"

Scale 1:6,250

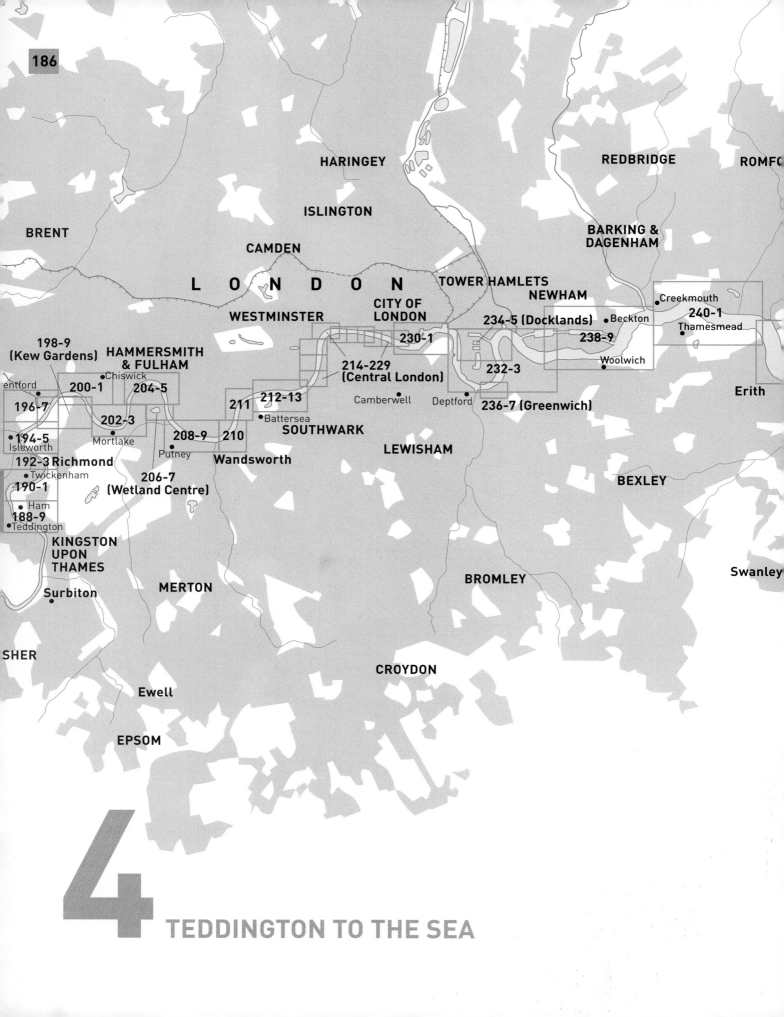

BASILDON

SOUTH
BENFLEET

Leigh-on-Sea

SOUTHEND-
ON-SEA

Westcliff-on-Sea

ꞏAVERING

Stanford-le-Hope

CANVEY
ISLAND

Coryton

Thames
Haven

250-1

•Mucking

nington
Aveley

Purfleet

West
Thurrock

Allhallows-
on-Sea

Dartford
Crossing
244-5

GRAYS

246-7

Tilbury

Halstow
Marshes

St
Mary's Marshes

Allhallows

Isle
of
Grain

•Cliffe

St Mary's Hoo

Lower Stoke

Greenhithe

Swanscombe

248-9

Church
Street

Stoke

Grain

Wallend

ꞏRTFORD

GRAVESEND

Medway

Strood

ROCHESTER

GILLINGHAM

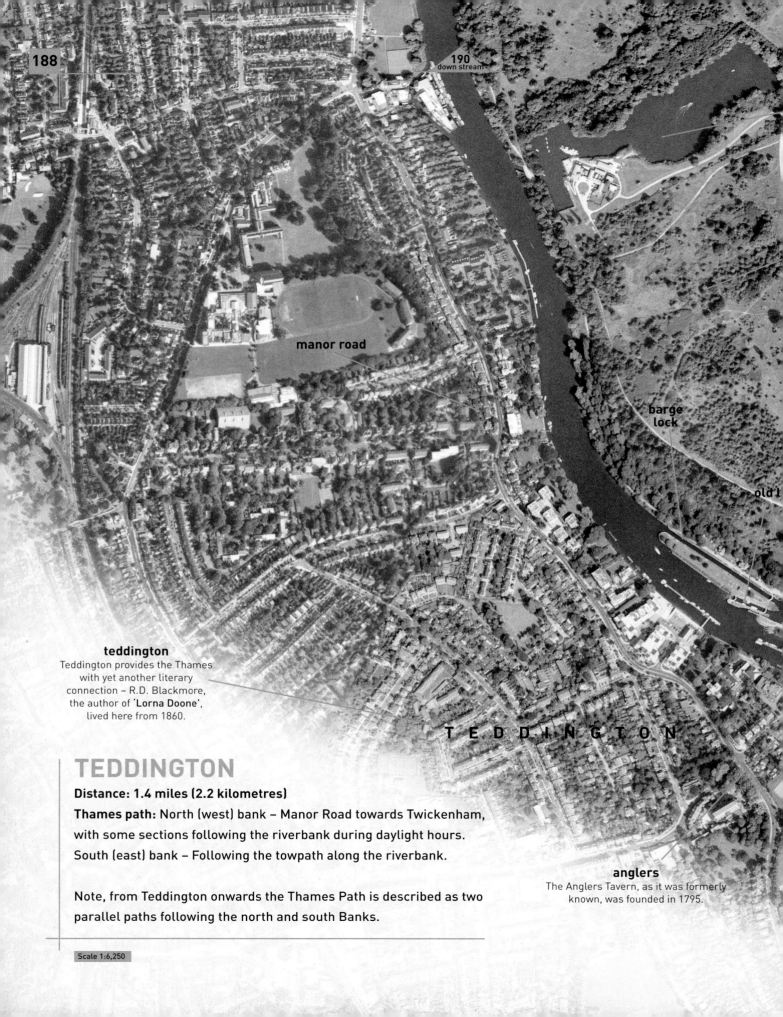

manor road

barge
lock

old l

teddington
Teddington provides the Thames
with yet another literary
connection – R.D. Blackmore,
the author of 'Lorna Doone',
lived here from 1860.

T E D D I N G T O N

TEDDINGTON

Distance: 1.4 miles (2.2 kilometres)

Thames path: North (west) bank – Manor Road towards Twickenham,
with some sections following the riverbank during daylight hours.
South (east) bank – Following the towpath along the riverbank.

Note, from Teddington onwards the Thames Path is described as two
parallel paths following the north and south Banks.

anglers
The Anglers Tavern, as it was formerly
known, was founded in 1795.

Scale 1:6,250

young mariners lock

ham lands

During the early 20th century much of Ham Lands was quarried for gravel, and the man-made lagoon of Young Mariners Lock was used for loading barges. After the Second World War, the quarries were filled with rubble from bomb-sites, creating Ham Lands, which is now a very rich plant habitat.

teddington locks

Teddington Lock is significant because, since 1811, it has done what Canute could not and held back the tide, forming the boundary between the tidal and non-tidal Thames. It is the biggest lock system on the river, with three locks of varying sizes: the tiny Skiff Lock, one of the smallest locks in Britain; a launch lock, known as the Old Lock; and the 198-metre Barge Lock, which has a third pair of gates that can reduce its size by half. The three locks are crossed by a footbridge, with a girder bridge crossing the lock cut itself and a suspension bridge over the weir stream.

H A M

skiff lock

footbridge 18' 4"

teddington weir

hames television studios

up stream
185

york house

This 17th-century riverside mansion takes its name from the Yorke family, which by then had been associated with Twickenham for some 300 years. In 1817, York House was bought by Anne Seymour Damer, sculptress of the masks of Thames and Isis on Henley Bridge (p.115), and the last private resident was Sir Ratan Tata, who built an exotic fountain in the grounds close to the river. York House now houses the municipal offices of the Borough of Richmond upon Thames.

orleans gardens and gallery

Orleans Gardens were once the grounds of Orleans House, which was built in 1710 but did not become known as Orleans House until after it had been used by the exiled Duke of Orléans from 1815–17. The last surviving part of the house is the Octagon, designed by James Gibbs in 1730, which now houses a free art gallery.

marble hill house

Built in 1723 for Henrietta Howard, the mistress of the future George II.

T W I C K E N H A M

barmy arms

A splendidly named pub that began life in 1727 as the Queen's Head. The current name is said to derive either from a barmy landlord or, more likely, from the froth on the top of fermenting ale, which is known as the barm.

eel pie island

With one of London's most evocative place-names, Eel Pie Island is home to about 300 people including a liberal smattering of artists, craftsmen and eccentrics – among whom is the island's most famous resident, inventor Trevor Bayliss. Until this century the island was only accessible by boat (it is now linked to Twickenham by a footbridge), and Henry VIII sailed here to sample the famous Eel Pies.

radnor gardens

up stream
188

Scale 1:6,250

192
down stream

marble hill park

horse reach

glover island

petersham meadows

hammerton's ferry
Ferry between Twickenham
and Richmond

P E T E R S H A M

ham house
Ham House was built in 1610 for Sir
Thomas Vavasour. Diarist John
Evelyn wrote of walking to Ham in
1678 'to see the House and Garden
of the Duke of Lauderdale, which is
indeed inferior to few of the best
Villas in Italy itself', and went on to
praise the gardens and the interior
which, he wrote, was 'furnished like
a great Prince's'.

EEL PIE ISLAND TO HORSE REACH

Distance: 1.7 miles (2.7 kilometres)
Thames path: North (west) bank – Riverside through Radnor
Gardens, then following Manor Road and rejoining the river opposite
Eel Pie Island. South (east) bank – Following the towpath along
the riverbank.

corporation island   duck's walk

twickenham
Twickenham, with its disputed placename meaning either 'land at the river fork' or 'Twicca's riverside land', remained very much a riverside village until the arrival of the railway in 1848, after which it expanded rapidly.

richmond bridge
An elegant five-arch masonry bridge faced in Portland stone, Richmond Bridge was designed by James Paine and Kenton Couse, and built from 1774–77.
17'4"

T W I C K E N H A M

TWICKENHAM AND RICHMOND

Distance: 0.6 miles (1.0 kilometres)

Thames path: North (west) bank – Following the riverbank to Richmond Bridge, then leaving the river and following Duck's Walk to rejoin the river at Richmond Railway Bridge.

South (east) bank – Following the riverbank.

Scale 1:3,125

richmond riverside
Richmond's main riverfront was redeveloped during the 1980s by architect Quinlan Terry, and opened by the Queen in 1988.

richmond
Henry VII was celebrating Christmas 1497 at Shene Palace when it was badly damaged by fire. Henry rebuilt the palace on a grand scale and, when it was completed in 1501, renamed it Richmond Palace after his earldom in Yorkshire. The town that was growing up immediately around the palace also took the new name of Richmond, although parts of the manor kept the name Shene, which survives today as Sheen (p.199).

RICHMOND

richmond hill
In 1727, Scottish poet James Thomson wrote of Richmond Hill: 'Heavens! What a goodly prospect spreads around, of hills, and dales, and woods, and lawn and spires and glittering towns and gilded streams.' The views remain spectacular today, if a little less rural.

up stream
191

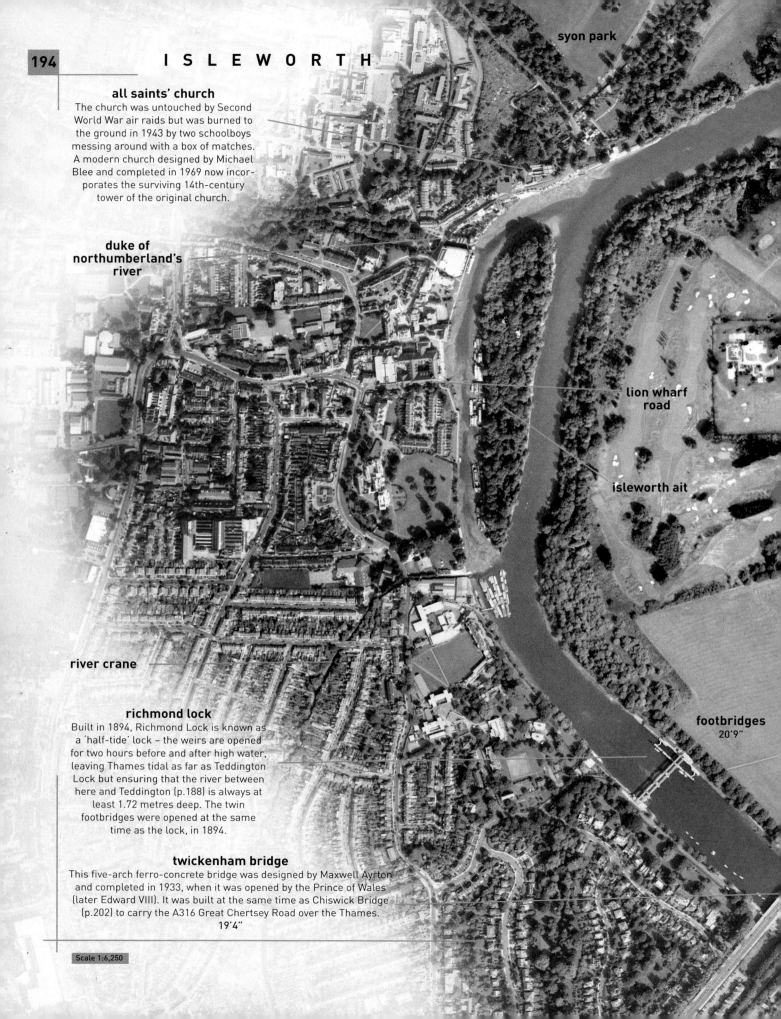

syon park

all saints' church
The church was untouched by Second World War air raids but was burned to the ground in 1943 by two schoolboys messing around with a box of matches. A modern church designed by Michael Blee and completed in 1969 now incorporates the surviving 14th-century tower of the original church.

duke of northumberland's river

lion wharf road

isleworth ait

river crane

richmond lock
Built in 1894, Richmond Lock is known as a 'half-tide' lock – the weirs are opened for two hours before and after high water, leaving Thames tidal as far as Teddington Lock but ensuring that the river between here and Teddington (p.188) is always at least 1.72 metres deep. The twin footbridges were opened at the same time as the lock, in 1894.

footbridges
20'9"

twickenham bridge
This five-arch ferro-concrete bridge was designed by Maxwell Ayrton and completed in 1933, when it was opened by the Prince of Wales (later Edward VIII). It was built at the same time as Chiswick Bridge (p.202) to carry the A316 Great Chertsey Road over the Thames.
19'4"

Scale 1:6,250

RICHMOND RAILWAY BRIDGE TO ISLEWORTH AIT

Distance: 1.9 miles (3.1 kilometres)

Thames path: North (west) bank – Riverbank to the River Crane, then following the main road to rejoin the river via Lion Wharf Road before leaving the river again at All Saints' Church to cut across Syon Park.

South (east) bank – Following the towpath along the riverbank.

kew observatory

The observatory was built by Sir William Chambers from 1768–69 for George III so that the king could watch the transit of Venus across the sun, which was due to take place on 3rd June 1769. The observatory was used by the Met Office until as late as 1981.

old deer park

The Old Deer Park was once exactly that. Its 250 acres now include the Royal Mid-Surrey Golf Course to the north and recreation grounds to the south.

richmond green

In 1849 Benjamin Disraeli, who later became Prime Minister, visited the Austrian statesman Metternich at Richmond and afterwards wrote:

'I am enchanted by Richmond Green, which, strange to say, I don't recollect ever having visited before, often as I have been to Richmond. I should like to let my house and live there. It is still and sweet, charming alike in summer and in winter.'

R I C H M O N D

richmond railway bridge

The present steel arch bridge was designed by J.W. Jacomb Hood and built in 1908 to replace the original cast-iron railway bridge of 1848.

17'4"

SYON PARK TO BRENTFORD AIT

Distance: 1.2 miles (1.9 kilometres)

Thames path: North bank – Through Syon Park, crossing the Grand Union Canal at High Street Bridge and continuing through Brentford to rejoin the river opposite Brentford Ait. South bank – Following the riverbank.

brentford

Brentford grew up not on the Thames but around a ford across the River Brent, hence the name. Brentford has been the scene of two battles: one in 1016 between Edmund Ironside and Cnut (aka Canute) and another in 1642 during the Civil War, when the Royalists prevailed and pressed on towards London only to be repelled at Turnham Green.

grand union canal

The Grand Union Canal was formed in 1929 as a huge network of canals incorporating the original Grand Union Canal (1814), the Grand Junction Canal, Regent's Canal and several others, linking London with Birmingham.

high street bridge

There has been a bridge on this site since at least as early as the 13th century. For much of its history it was known as Brentford Bridge.

syon house

Syon House was built during the 16th century by Edward Seymour, Duke of Somerset, and it was remodelled by Inigo Jones in the 17th century and Robert Adam in the 18th. The first two owners were both executed – the Duke of Somerset for felony and the next owner, John Dudley, Duke of Northumberland, for offering the crown to his daughter-in-law Lady Jane Grey, who became known as the 'nine days queen'. After Dudley's demise the property reverted to the Crown and was later granted by Elizabeth I to the Percys, Earls and later Dukes of Northumberland, whose home it has been since 1594.

butterfly house and reptile house

Scale 1:6,250

BRENTFORD

W R S

brentford ait

river brent

**brentford dock
marina**

syon park
Laid out by Capability Brown
during the 18th century, Syon Park
was opened to the pubic in 1837.

kew gardens
see pages 198-199.

10

5

6

2

9

3

4

8

Scale 1:6,250

ROYAL BOTANIC GARDENS, KEW

royal botanic gardens, kew

Kew Gardens began life as a pleasure garden created in 1731 by Prince Frederick, the eldest son of George II. Frederick died in 1751 after being hit by a cricket ball and it was his widow, Princess Augusta (mother of George III), who established the first botanic garden at Kew in 1759. Some of its earliest specimens were brought back from the voyages of Captain Cook, establishing Kew from the start as a centre for botanical research. The original nine-acre garden was later united with the grounds of Richmond Lodge (landscaped by Capability Brown) and, with botanist Sir Joseph Banks as unofficial director, Kew Gardens became famous. The gardens were handed to the nation by Royal Commission in 1840 and a year later Sir William Hooker was appointed the first official director. The Royal Botanic Gardens now covers 300 acres and exhibits more than 33,000 plant species.

princess of wales conservatory (1)

The Princess of Wales Conservatory was designed by Gordon Wilson and opened in 1987.

palm house (2)

The Palm House was designed by architect Decimus Burton with engineer Richard Turner, and built from 1844–48.

temperate house (3)

The Temperate House, which is the largest of Kew's glasshouses, was designed by Decimus Burton and built from 1860–99.

queen's cottage (4)

Queen's Cottage was built c. 1771 for George III's queen, Charlotte. The cottage was given to the nation by Queen Victoria on her Diamond Jubilee in 1897, and was first opened to the public in 1899.

orangery (5)

waterlily house (6)

the pond (7)

pagoda (8)

the lake (9)

kew palace (10)

Formerly known as the Dutch House, this riverside mansion was built in 1631 and became a favourite retreat of George II after it had been leased by his queen, Caroline, in 1728. In 1818, the Prince Regent ordered the demolition of the Dutch House but the order was suspended and the house survived, becoming known as the Old Palace and lastly as Kew Palace. Elizabeth II opened the garden of Kew Palace to the public in 1969.

kew bridge
The present three-arch granite bridge was designed by architect Sir John Wolfe-Barry and engineer Cuthbert Brereton, and opened in 1903 by Edward VII – it is officially known as the King Edward VII bridge, after the new king who had been crowned the previous year. There had been two previous bridges here, the first one built from 1758–59.
17'4"

brentford ait

strand on the green
Time seems to have passed by this picturesque parade of rustic cottages, which includes almshouses dating from 1724, and Zoffany House, home for more than 30 years to artist John Zoffany.

bell & crown
This pub was first licensed in 1751, although the present building dates only from 1907. The pub sign depicts smugglers bringing goods into the Bell & Crown from the Port of London further downstream.

197 up stream

kew pier

oliver's ait

city barge
The City Barge dates back to 1484 when it was known as the Navigator's Arms, and is so much a Thames pub that it has a water-tight door which is kept firmly closed when high tides are due. It gained its present name during the 18th century, when the Lord Mayor of London's barge was moored nearby.

kew railway bridge
This five-span iron lattice girder bridge was built from 1864–69 by W.R. Galbraith for the London & South Western Railway.
18'4"

hartington road
(thames path)

BRENTFORD AIT TO CHISWICK

Distance: 0.9 miles (1.5 kilometres)

Thames path: North bank – Following the riverbank and then veering away from the river along Hartington Road, rejoining the river at Chiswick Bridge (p.202).

South bank – Following the towpath along the riverbank.

chiswick

Chiswick has something of an identity crisis because it is not known whether the name means Cheese Farm or Village by the Stony Beach. Chiswick has never been heavily industrial but John Thornycroft started his now world-renowned shipbuilding business here in 1866 before moving to Southampton in 1904.

C H I S W I C K

chiswick house

Like Palladio's Villa Rotunda near Vicenza that inspired it, Chiswick House was intended to be a 'temple to the arts'. It was built during the 1720s by the 3rd Earl of Burlington who, as well as charging visitors an admission fee to view his collection, would entertain his friends here, including Swift, Handel and Alexander Pope who lived nearby in Twickenham. The house is now managed by English Heritage.

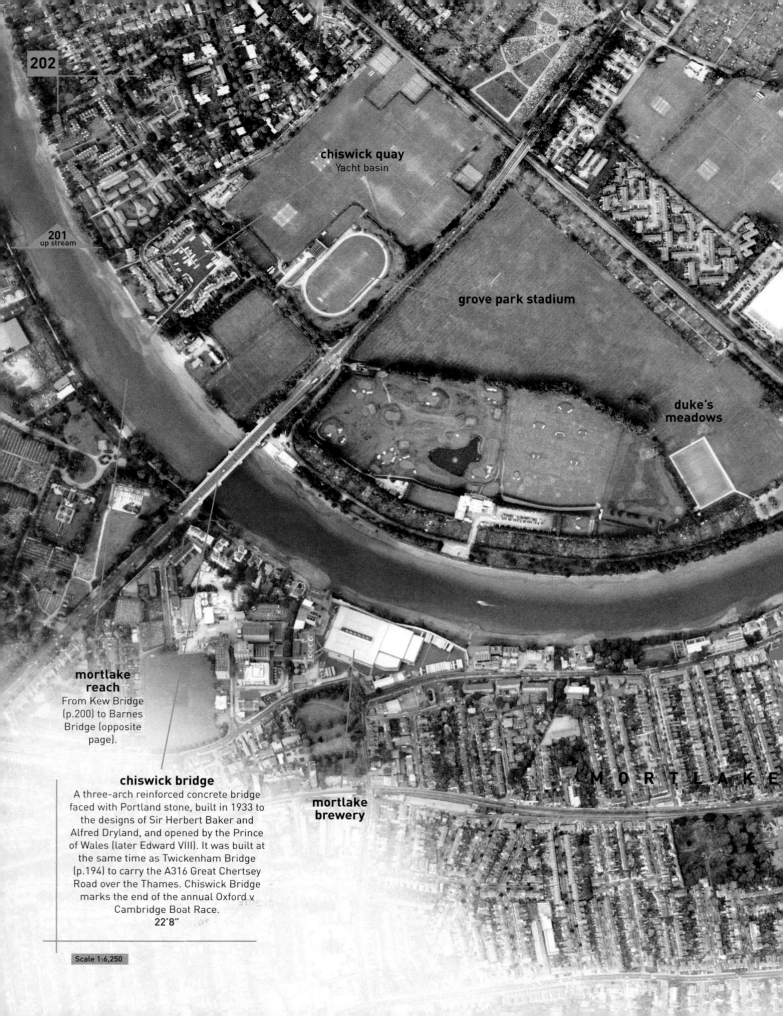

chiswick quay
Yacht basin

201
up stream

grove park stadium

duke's
meadows

mortlake
reach
From Kew Bridge
(p.200) to Barnes
Bridge (opposite
page).

chiswick bridge
A three-arch reinforced concrete bridge
faced with Portland stone, built in 1933 to
the designs of Sir Herbert Baker and
Alfred Dryland, and opened by the Prince
of Wales (later Edward VIII). It was built at
the same time as Twickenham Bridge
(p.194) to carry the A316 Great Chertsey
Road over the Thames. Chiswick Bridge
marks the end of the annual Oxford v
Cambridge Boat Race.
22'8"

mortlake
brewery

M O R T L A K E

Scale 1:6,250

corney reach
From Barnes Bridge to
Hammersmith Bridge (p.205).

204
down stream

203

B A R N E S

barnes common
The common was drained during the
19th century and extends to about 120
acres.

barnes bridge
An elegant iron railway bridge designed by
Joseph Locke for the London & South
Western Railway and built in 1846–49. It was
reconstructed in 1891–95 when a new
wrought-iron bridge was built alongside on
the downstream side.
17'9"

barnes terrace
A terrace of 18th-and 19th-century houses
once occupied by luminaries including
Gustav Holst, who lived at No 10 while he
was Director of Music at St Paul's Girls'
School, Hammersmith.

MORTLAKE REACH TO CORNEY REACH

Distance: 1.5 miles (2.4 kilometres)

Thames path: North bank – following the riverside with a slight detour to pass
under the railway. South bank – following the riverside.

CORNEY REACH TO BARN ELMS REACH

Distance: 2.3 miles (3.8 kilometres)

Thames path: North bank – Following the riverbank, with slight

deviations. South bank – Following the towpath along the riverbank.

fuller's brewery
More correctly known as Fuller, Smith and Turner's Griffin Brewery, Fuller's continues a tradition of brewing on this site that dates back to the time of Elizabeth I.

hammersmith terrace
A terrace of 17 identical houses built during the mid-18th century. Thames historian A. P. Herbert lived in this terrace within sight of his beloved river.

chiswick ayot

hogarth roundabout
A name infamous to anyone who listens to the traffic news, the Hogarth Roundabout is characterised by the frail-looking single-lane flyover that carries through traffic on the A316 over the roundabout on its spindly steel legs. The roundabout takes its name from Hogarth's House 50 yards to the west, which was the country retreat where William Hogarth and his family came to find peace and quiet each summer from 1749 until 1764.

corney reach
From Barnes Bridge (p.203) to Hammersmith Bridge

church of st nicolas
St Nicolas was the patron saint of sailors and fisherman, and the dedication of this church to him is a reminder that Chiswick was once a fishing village. The tower dates from 1446 but the rest of the building was rebuilt in 1882 by J. L. Pearson. The painter William Hogarth, who lived nearby, is buried in the churchyard.

Scale 1:6,250

hammersmith

Since Anglo–Saxon times, Hammersmith has been dominated by the roads along which it developed, a fact which still holds true today – the Hammersmith Flyover was built in 1961 to relieve congestion on Hammersmith Broadway, which was one of the busiest traffic intersections in London.

hammersmith bridge

The original Hammersmith Bridge was designed by William Tierney Clarke and built from 1824–27 as the first suspension bridge to be built in London. Sir Joseph Bazalgette replaced Tierney's bridge in 1883–87 with a very similar suspension bridge, which has twice been the target of IRA bomb attacks.

12'2"

the dove

hammersmith pier

rutland

blue anchor

riverside studios

harrods depository

This famous building is to the Boat Race commentary what the Hogarth Roundabout is to traffic reports. But the title is now a misnomer because, behind its familiar façade, the Harrods Depository has been given over to apartments.

barn elms reach

From Hammersmith Bridge to Putney Bridge (p.208).

wetland centre
see pages 206–207

down stream
207

WETLAND CENTRE

Distance: 0.5 miles
(0.8 kilometres)
Thames path: West and east
banks – following the riverside.

WETLAND CENTRE

The 105 acres of the Wetland Centre were laid out from 1995–2000 by the Wetland Advisory Agency, and opened on 26th May 2000 as a sanctuary for wetland birds whose natural habitat is fast disappearing. The Barn Elms reservoirs, already designated a Site of Special Scientific Interest, became redundant after the building of Thames Water's London Tunnel Ring Main (a 50-mile tunnel 130 feet below ground) and the Wildfowl and Wetlands Trust intervened to transform the concrete reservoirs into an urban wetland reserve. Sir David Attenborough described the resulting Wetland Centre as 'an ideal model for how the natural world and humanity might exist alongside one another in the centuries to come.'

BARNES

Scale 1:3,125

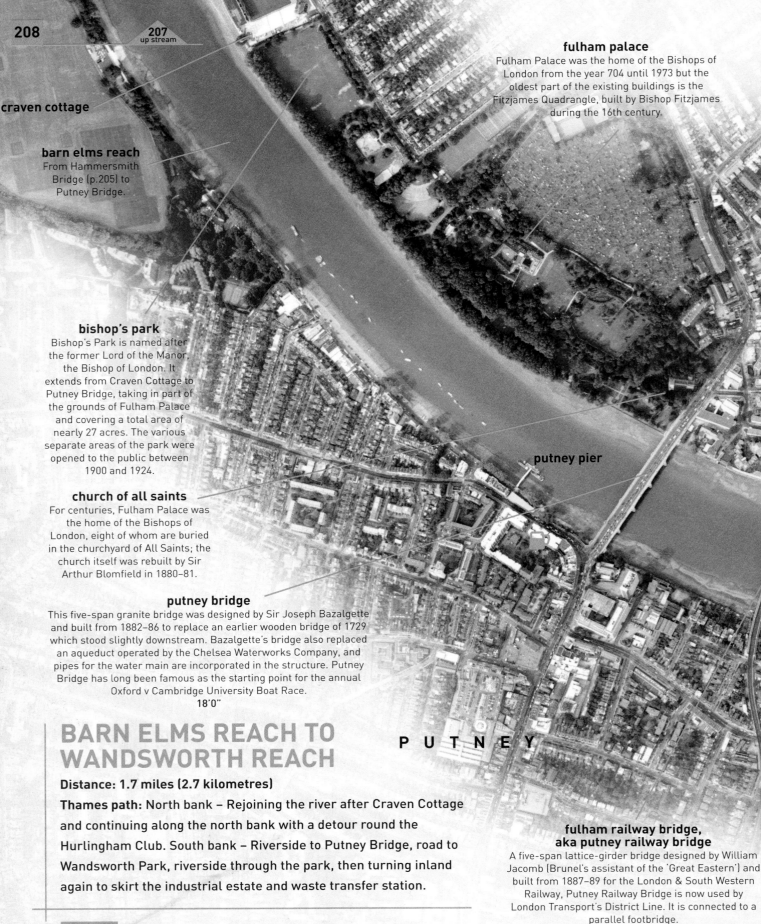

207
up stream

craven cottage

barn elms reach
From Hammersmith
Bridge (p.205) to
Putney Bridge.

fulham palace
Fulham Palace was the home of the Bishops of
London from the year 704 until 1973 but the
oldest part of the existing buildings is the
Fitzjames Quadrangle, built by Bishop Fitzjames
during the 16th century.

bishop's park
Bishop's Park is named after
the former Lord of the Manor,
the Bishop of London. It
extends from Craven Cottage to
Putney Bridge, taking in part of
the grounds of Fulham Palace
and covering a total area of
nearly 27 acres. The various
separate areas of the park were
opened to the public between
1900 and 1924.

putney pier

church of all saints
For centuries, Fulham Palace was
the home of the Bishops of
London, eight of whom are buried
in the churchyard of All Saints; the
church itself was rebuilt by Sir
Arthur Blomfield in 1880–81.

putney bridge
This five-span granite bridge was designed by Sir Joseph Bazalgette
and built from 1882–86 to replace an earlier wooden bridge of 1729
which stood slightly downstream. Bazalgette's bridge also replaced
an aqueduct operated by the Chelsea Waterworks Company, and
pipes for the water main are incorporated in the structure. Putney
Bridge has long been famous as the starting point for the annual
Oxford v Cambridge University Boat Race.
18'0"

BARN ELMS REACH TO
WANDSWORTH REACH

P U T N E Y

Distance: 1.7 miles (2.7 kilometres)

Thames path: North bank – Rejoining the river after Craven Cottage
and continuing along the north bank with a detour round the
Hurlingham Club. South bank – Riverside to Putney Bridge, road to
Wandsworth Park, riverside through the park, then turning inland
again to skirt the industrial estate and waste transfer station.

Scale 1:6,250

**fulham railway bridge,
aka putney railway bridge**
A five-span lattice-girder bridge designed by William
Jacomb (Brunel's assistant of the 'Great Eastern') and
built from 1887–89 for the London & South Western
Railway, Putney Railway Bridge is now used by
London Transport's District Line. It is connected to a
parallel footbridge.
22'7"

fulham

Until it was built up during the 19th century, Fulham was known as 'the great fruit and kitchen garden north of the Thames', with a high street that led to a ferry across the river.

hurlingham club

Hurlingham House was built in 1760 for a Dr William Cadogan and now forms the centrepiece of the Hurlingham Club. In 1867 the house was leased by Frank Heathcote, who set up a pigeon-shooting club; the club's activities extended to polo, and in 1875 the rules of the sport were formalised by the Hurlingham Club Committee. The polo grounds were compulsorily purchased by the London County Council in 1946 for housing but this exclusive club still boasts extensive sports facilities.

south park

hurlingham park

F U L H A M

wandsworth reach

From Putney Bridge to Wandsworth Bridge (p.210).

river wandle

waste transfer station

An overhead walkway will eventually carry the Thames Path over this vast transfer station and recycling centre.

210 down stream

wandsworth park

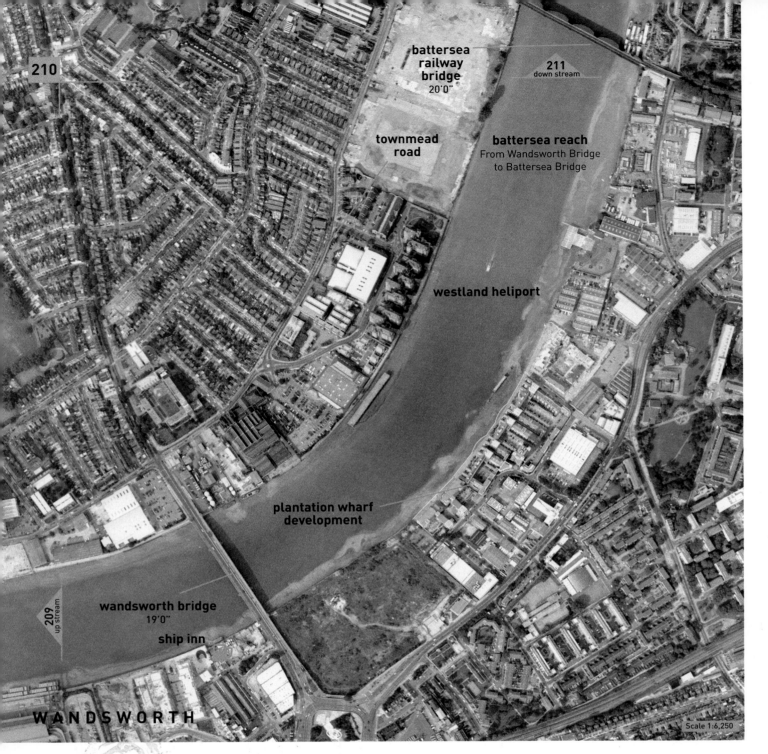

battersea
railway
bridge
20'0"

211
down stream

townmead
road

battersea reach
From Wandsworth Bridge
to Battersea Bridge

westland heliport

plantation wharf
development

209
up stream

wandsworth bridge
19'0"

ship inn

WANDSWORTH

Scale 1:6,250

WANDSWORTH TO BATTERSEA RAILWAY BRIDGE

Distance: 0.9 miles (1.4 kilometres)

Thames path: North bank – Leaves the river at Wandsworth Bridge, following Townmead Road to rejoin the river at Chelsea Harbour (p. 211). South bank – Along the road from Wandsworth Bridge to Battersea Railway Bridge.

battersea railway bridge

A five-span wrought-iron bridge built from 1861–63 to carry the West London Extension Railway, a short but extremely important line linking the trunk lines approaching London from the north and west with those approaching from the south and south-east, allowing direct connections between north and south. Before its 'Extension', the West London Railway was ridiculed so often in 'Punch' magazine that it became known as Mr Punch's Railway.

wandsworth bridge

A three-span steel bridge built from 1936–40 to the designs of Sir T. Pierson Frank, with E. P. Wheeler and F. R. Hiorns as architectural consultants.

BATTERSEA RAILWAY BRIDGE TO ALBERT BRIDGE

Distance: 1.1 miles (1.7 kilometres)

Thames path: North bank – In front of Chelsea Harbour, behind Lots Road Power Station, continuing along Cheyne Walk. South bank – Following the riverbank.

battersea bridge
Another bridge by the prolific Victorian engineer Sir Joseph Bazalgette, the present five-span cast-iron Battersea Bridge was built from 1886–90 to replace an earlier wooden structure that featured in the paintings of Whistler and Turner.

albert bridge
Providing one of London's most picturesque river crossings, Albert Bridge is a three-span 'straight link' suspension bridge built by R. M. Ordish from 1871–73.
16'0"

Scale 1:6,250

cadogan pier

212 down stream

lots road power station

chelsea creek

chelsea harbour
P&O describes its 1980s marina and luxury development at Chelsea Harbour as 'a unique world of houses, flats, offices, restaurants and a luxury hotel around a working yacht harbour'.
The blurb may be accurate but the name is not – the southern boundary of Chelsea is formed by Chelsea Creek, to the north of Chelsea Harbour, which means that the entire harbour complex lies not in Chelsea but in Fulham.

cheyne walk
Before the construction in 1871 of the embankment that now carries the busy A3212 past Cheyne Walk, the elegant houses stood on the peaceful Thames foreshore, attracting residents such as Whistler, Turner, Wilson Steer, Dante Gabriel Rossetti, Swinburne, Henry James, George Eliot and Hilaire Belloc. Their legacy is a huge number of blue plaques looking forlornly at the river across a busy, heavily polluted swathe of tarmac.

up stream
210

CHELSEA

royal hospital,
chelsea

grosvenor canal basin

chelsea bridge
21'8"

chelsea reach
From Battersea Bridge to
Chelsea Bridge (p.212)

chelsea physic garden   children's zoo

211
up stream

peace pagoda

The Peace Pagoda was accepted as a gift from the
Nipponzan Myohoji Order of Buddhists by the Greater
London Council in 1984 as part of their Peace Year. It was
completed in 1985 and is one of 70 such pagodas to be built
around the world in the name of peace.

battersea park

Battersea Park, which now covers 198 acres, was laid out
by Sir James Pennethorne and opened in 1853. Prior to
that the area had been a series of low marshes, streams
and ditches known as Battersea Fields: the soil used for
consolidating this marshland came from the excavation of
the Royal Victoria Dock further downstream (p.233).

CHELSEA REACH TO NINE ELMS REACH

Distance: 1.6 miles (2.6 kilometres)

Thames path: North bank – Following the riverfront. South bank – Riverfront through
Battersea Park, then diverting inland to skirt Battersea Power Station via Nine Elms
Road before returning to the riverfront.

Scale 1:6,250

grosvenor railway bridge
This is two bridges masquerading as one. The twin four-arch bridges were built in 1858–60 and 1865–66 for two different railway companies, both serving Victoria Station, and were known collectively as Victoria Bridge. Now known as Grosvenor Bridge, they were rebuilt in 1963–67, when the original wrought-iron piers were encased in concrete.
19'8"

P I M L I C O

vauxhall bridge
18'4"

nine elms reach
From Chelsea Bridge to Vauxhall Bridge

nine elms road

N I N E   E L M S

nine elms
Since Nine Elms was first named in 1645 after a row of trees bordering the road, it has been an industrial area, developing from lime kilns and potteries through gasworks, waterworks and railway yards to new factory units and warehouses.

new covent garden market
The original fruit, flower and vegetable market had been established in Covent Garden for more than 300 years before it moved in 1974 to this 68-acre site on land formerly owned by British Rail.

royal hospital, chelsea
The Royal Hospital, Chelsea, aka the Chelsea Hospital, was founded by Charles II and built from 1682–92 by Sir Christopher Wren. Legend has it that Charles II was persuaded to found this famous hospital by Nell Gwyn but, while it is true that she was one of the hospital's first patrons, it is more likely that Charles was emulating the example of Louis XIV's Hotel des Invalides in Paris. The first of the famous Chelsea Pensioners took up residence in 1689, three years before the hospital was completed, and more than three centuries later Chelsea Pensioners can still be identified by the same distinctive red uniform.

battersea power station
Battersea Power Station was designed by Sir Giles Gilbert Scott. Station A opened in 1933 with one chimney at each end, and the station was later doubled in size with the addition of Station B to the east which, although it began generating power in 1948, was not completed until 1953. The power station was decommissioned in 1983 and five years later the site was re-opened for development as a leisure park but it was abandoned again in 1991 after the developer ran out of money.

thames house

millbank
tower

lambeth reach
From Vauxhall Bridge
to Westminster Bridge
(pp 218–19).

tate britain

millbank

vauxhall bridge
18'4"

Scale 1:3,125

lfcda pier

tate britain

Tate Britain was built on the site of the notorious Millbank Penitentiary and opened in 1897 as the National Gallery of British Art using money donated by sugar magnate Sir Henry Tate, who also donated his collection of 65 paintings and two sculptures. The gallery houses the largest Turner collection in the world and sponsors the prestigious, and usually controversial, Turner Prize, **(opposite page)**.

albert embankment

The Albert Embankment is an amazing feat of engineering by the Victorian engineer Sir Joseph Bazalgette, who also built a number of other bridges across the Thames. It was built from 1866–70 on land reclaimed from the river by constructing two walls, one extending several metres below the low-water mark and another several metres above the high.

millbank tower

Built from 1960–63 by architects Ronald Ward & Partners for the Vickers Group, this 387-ft office building has recently achieved listed status. The tower provided the eyrie from which Oskar Kokoshka painted his riverscape **'View of the Thames from the Vickers Building, Millbank'** in 1962, before the building was even completed. The tower was the headquarters of the Labour Party from 1997–2002. **(opposite page)**.

mi6

The headquarters of MI6 is not exactly secretive, and even makes an appearance in a James Bond film. Seen from the air, the depth of architect Terry Farrell's postmodernist ziggurat is surprising compared with the foreshortened view to be had on the ground.

vauxhall bridge

Regent's Bridge, as it was then known, opened in 1816 as London's first iron bridge over the Thames, designed by James Walker. It was replaced in 1895–1906 by the present five-arch steel bridge designed by Sir Alexander Binnie, with bronze figures by F. W. Pomeroy and Alfred Drury. **(opposite page)**.

VAUXHALL BRIDGE TO LAMBETH BRIDGE

Distance: 0.5 miles (0.8 kilometres)
Thames path: North (west) bank – Along Millbank, following the riverfront. South (east) bank – Along the Albert Embankment, following the riverfront.

V A U X H A L L

216

westminster abbey

Since St Peter apocryphally came here to dedicate the church that bore his name, what is now Westminster Abbey has played a large role in the history of England. Rebuilt by King Canute, Edward the Confessor and Henry III, the cathedral has seen the coronation of every English monarch since William the Conqueror (except for Edward V and Edward VIII, neither of whom was crowned) and the burial of every monarch in the 500 years between Henry III and George II.

victoria tower

The Sovereign's Entrance, used by the monarch at the State Opening of Parliament, is at the base of the 330-ft Victoria Tower. The tower was completed in 1860, eight years after parliament began meeting in these new buildings, and it is now used as the repository for parliamentary records.

victoria tower gardens

The gardens include a replica of Rodin's sculpture 'Burghers of Calais', a Gothic fountain commemorating the emancipation of slaves in the British Empire, and a statue by A. G. Walker of suffragette Emmeline Pankhurst.

LAMBETH BRIDGE TO WESTMINSTER BRIDGE

Distance: 0.4 miles (0.7 kilometres)

Thames path: North Bank – Through Victoria Tower Gardens, following the road to the west of the Palace of Westminster to rejoin the river at Westminster Bridge. South Bank – Along the Albert Embankment and under Lambeth Bridge, continuing along the riverfront.

Scale 1:3,125

219
down stream

westminster bridge
17'8"

big ben

houses of parliament

lambeth reach
From Vauxhall Bridge
to Westminster Bridge
(pp 218-219).

victoria tower

lambeth pier

archbishop's park

up stream
215

big ben

Mike McCann, the current Keeper of the Great Clock, says 'I once read that Big Ben is the most widely recognised building on the planet' and yet, like so many of London's towers, it is known by the incorrect name. 'Big Ben' is actually the name of the 13.5-ton hour bell which hangs in what is officially known as the Clock Tower.

st thomas's hospital

houses of parliament

The Houses of Parliament are officially known as the Palace of Westminster. The first palace here was built by King Canute, and the Palace of Westminster remained the official residence of the reigning monarch and his court until it was abandoned by Henry VIII in 1532, after which parliament continued to meet at Westminster, which meant that for the first time in history the monarch's residence and the administrative centre of the kingdom were separated. Three centuries later, on 16th October 1834, the palace burned to the ground. It was rebuilt from 1840–60 by Sir Charles Barry, with ornamentation by Augustus Pugin, as a purpose-built home for both Houses of Parliament, with an amazing 1,000 rooms linked by two miles of corridors.

lambeth palace

The official residence of the Archbishop of Canterbury. Hubert Walter was the first archbishop to live here, acquiring the Manor in 1197 and building Lambeth House shortly afterwards. The house was much extended by successive archbishops, and was known as Lambeth Palace by the time Archbishop Matthew Parker died here in 1575. Parker, who is buried in the chapel at Lambeth Palace, was notorious for meddling in state affairs and is thought to be the original 'nosey Parker'.

lambeth bridge

Historic crossings at this point included a horse ferry, which was a large raft-like craft designed to carry a horse-drawn carriage complete with passengers and which gave its name to nearby Horseferry Road. The ferry closed down after the construction of Westminster Bridge (top of picture), and it was eventually replaced by a temporary wooden footbridge and then the first Lambeth Bridge: a suspension footbridge built from 1861–62 by P. W. Barlow. This in turn was replaced by the present five-span steel-arch bridge, built by Sir Charles George Humphreys and Sir Reginald Blomfield and opened by George V in 1932.
21'4"

WESTMINSTER BRIDGE TO HUNGERFORD BRIDGE

Distance: 0.4 miles (0.7 kilometres)

Thames path: North and south banks – Following the embankments along the riverfront.

downing street

The most famous address in British politics was built by an American: New Englander George Downing built fifteen houses on Downing Street, of which just three survive. Some of the houses were taken over as offices after the destruction of Whitehall Palace by fire in 1694, and No10 became the Treasury Office. In 1732 George II offered a large house backing on to No10 as a personal gift to Sir Robert Walpole, the First Lord of the Treasury, but Walpole would only accept it in his official capacity for holders of the office. Since then No10, including the L-shaped Lichfield House annexe (which is connected to No10 by a long corridor), has been the official residence of the Prime Minister – a post still officially known as First Lord of the Treasury.

foreign & commonwealth office

The Foreign and Commonwealth Office, more popularly known simply as the Foreign Office, or FO, now occupies the whole of a building originally built to house the Foreign, India, Home and Colonial Offices.

westminster bridge

The present seven-arch iron bridge was built from 1854–62 by Thomas Page and Sir Charles Barry, and replaces the one on which Wordsworth stood when the view inspired him to write his poem 'Lines Written Upon Westminster Bridge':

'Earth has not anything to show more fair,
Dull would he be of soul who could pass by,
A sight so touching in its majesty...'

victoria embankment

Begun slightly earlier than the Albert Embankment (p.215), the Victoria Embankment was built by Sir Joseph Bazalgette from 1864-70, reclaiming 37 acres of land from the river.

Scale 1:3,125

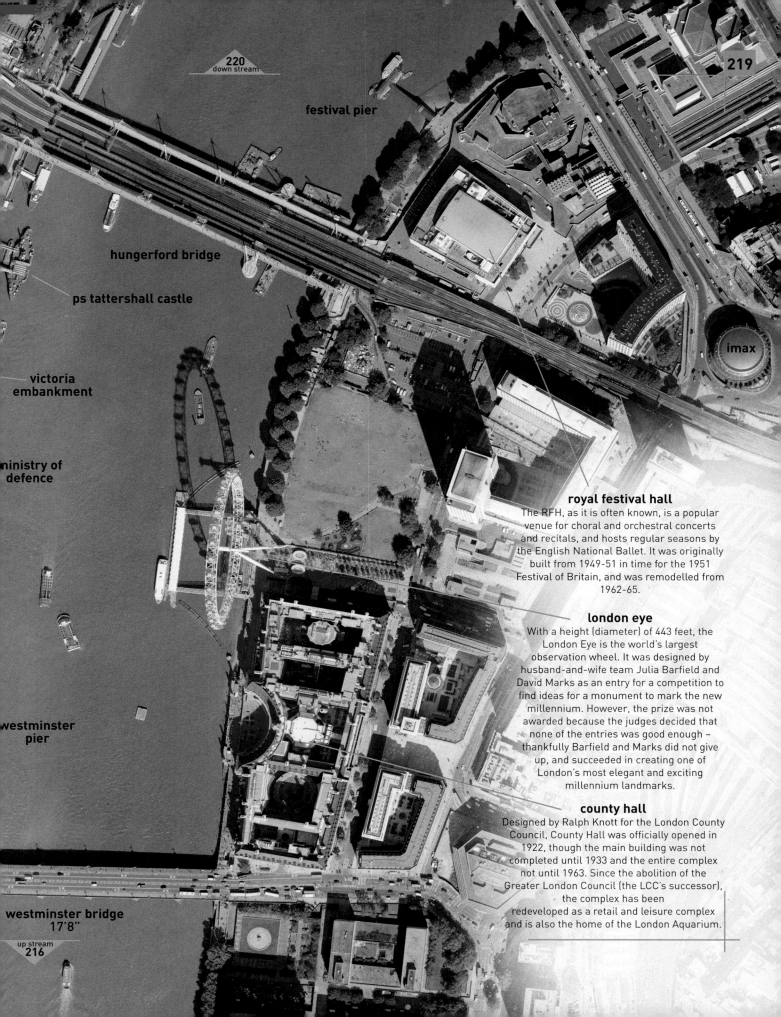

festival pier

imax

hungerford bridge

ps tattershall castle

victoria
embankment

ministry of
defence

westminster
pier

westminster bridge
17'8"

royal festival hall

The RFH, as it is often known, is a popular venue for choral and orchestral concerts and recitals, and hosts regular seasons by the English National Ballet. It was originally built from 1949-51 in time for the 1951 Festival of Britain, and was remodelled from 1962-65.

london eye

With a height (diameter) of 443 feet, the London Eye is the world's largest observation wheel. It was designed by husband-and-wife team Julia Barfield and David Marks as an entry for a competition to find ideas for a monument to mark the new millennium. However, the prize was not awarded because the judges decided that none of the entries was good enough – thankfully Barfield and Marks did not give up, and succeeded in creating one of London's most elegant and exciting millennium landmarks.

county hall

Designed by Ralph Knott for the London County Council, County Hall was officially opened in 1922, though the main building was not completed until 1933 and the entire complex not until 1963. Since the abolition of the Greater London Council (the LCC's successor), the complex has been redeveloped as a retail and leisure complex and is also the home of the London Aquarium.

220

savoy hotel

cleopatra's needle

charing cross pier

up stream
219

festival pier

Scale 1:6,250

king's college

hqs wellington

222
down stream

7

6

CHARING CROSS STATION TO HQS WELLINGTON

Distance: 0.6 miles (0.9 kilometres)
Thames path: North and south banks – Following the embankments along the riverfront.

charing cross station and embankment place (1)
The original station was designed by John Hawkshaw and opened in 1864. The single-arch roof of the trainshed collapsed during maintenance in 1905, killing six men and destroying the Avenue Theatre next door, which has since been rebuilt as The Playhouse. The replacement roof was later demolished to make way for Embankment Place, Terry Farrell's spectacular office complex built above the station in 1999, which was designed to evoke the ethos of the Victorian trainshed but has been said to resemble anenormous jukebox.

victoria embankment gardens (2)
The buildings lining the northern edge of the gardens stand where the river bank once was, and the water at high tide would have covered the area where the road and the gardens are now.

waterloo bridge (3)
John Rennie's original Waterloo Bridge (1811–17) was described by parliament as 'a work of stability and magnificence' but it proved not to be so: in 1923, two of the piers settled and a temporary bridge had to be built alongside. Both were demolished in 1936 and replaced by the present 5-arch concrete bridge, which was designed by Sir Giles Gilbert Scott and built from 1937–42.
27'10"

aldwych (4)
The distinctive 'D' of Aldwych forms the crescent link between the Strand and Kingsway. It was conceived as part of the last great Victorian metropolitan improvement scheme, although it was Victoria's successor who officiated at the opening ceremony – in 1905 Edward VII declared the development open, and Kingsway was named in his honour.

somerset house (5)
The present building stands on the site of a 16th century palace, and was built from 1776 by William Chambers for government offices. Instead it became the home of the Royal Academy, the Royal Society and the Society of Antiquaries and then, until 1973, the Registry of Births, Deaths and Marriages. It is now the home of the Courtauld Institute and Gilbert Collection Galleries, and the courtyard is used in the winter months as a public ice rink.

london studios (6)
Studios of London Weekend Television.

royal national theatre (7)
The idea of a national theatre was first mooted in 1848 but the National Theatre Company was not founded until 1962, and the building itself, designed by Denys Lasdun and built from 1951–77, did not open until 1976, with a performance of Albert Finney's **'Hamlet'**.

TEMPLE TO BANKSIDE

Distance: 0.7 miles (1.2 kilometres)

Thames path: North and south banks – Following the embankment along the riverfront.

inner & middle temple (1)

Temple has been at the heart of the legal profession since the 13th century, when four Inns of Court were established as places where prospective lawyers could eat, sleep and study. Temple comprises two Inns, Middle Temple and Inner Temple, which were originally hostels built by the Knights Templar. A few of the medieval buildings survive, including Temple Church (1185), but most of the current buildings were rebuilt during the 1950s after being heavily bombed in the Blitz.

gabriel's wharf (2)

The Coin Street Community rescued Gabriel's Wharf from commercial development and turned it into a relaxed plaza of craft shops, bars, brasseries and a week-end craft market.

oxo tower (3)

This art deco tower stands on the site of an old power station which was converted into a meat-packing factory by the makers of OXO cubes. In order to circumvent a ban on illuminated advertisements, architect Albert Moore incorporated the letters o-x-o into the windows of the tower so that they would be lit from within.

doggett's coat & badge pub (4)

The pub dates only from 1976 but the name goes right back to the 18th century, when actor-manager Thomas Doggett of the Drury Lane Theatre set up what is now the country's longest-running annual sporting event, a sculling race for apprentice Watermen known as the Doggett's Coat and Badge Race. The prize – a coat and badge.

blackfriars bridge (5)

The present 5-arch wrought iron bridge was designed by Joseph Cubitt and H. Carr, built from 1860-69, and opened by Queen Victoria. The bridge was widened by 35 feet, from 1907-10.
23'0"

blackfriars railway bridges (6)

The western bridge was built in 1862-64 to carry the London, Chatham & Dover Railway over the river, designed by Joseph Cubitt and F. T. Turner to be in architectural harmony with Cubitt's road bridge just upstream. Only the piers of this bridge remain because it was replaced by the 5-arch eastern bridge, built from 1884-86 to the designs of John Wolfe-Barry and H. M. Brunel to carry the railway into what was then called St Paul's Station but which was renamed Blackfriars Station in 1937.
23'0"

bankside gallery (7)

The Bankside Gallery, close to Tate Modern, is the home of the Royal Watercolour Society, which was founded in 1804, and the Royal Society of Painter Printmakers, which was founded in 1880. The gallery provides a showcase for works of art painted or printed by members of both Societies.

hqs wellington

hms presider

king's reach
From Westminster Bridge (pp.218-219) to London Bridge (p.225).

221
up stream

blackfriars
pier

blackfriars
station

city of london
school

5

6

224
down
stream

queen's walk

3

4

7

223

city of london
school

2

queen's walk

bankside
jetty

4

3

1

Scale 1:3,125

swan lane pier

clink prison
museum

BANKSIDE TO SWAN LANE PIER

Distance: 0.7 miles (1.2 kilometres)
Thames path: North bank – Following the embankment along the riverfront. South bank – Riverfront as far as Cannon Street Bridge, veering away from the river to skirt the precinct of Southwark Cathedral, rejoining the river just east of London Bridge.

tate modern (1)
At the turn of the 21st century, Sir Giles Gilbert Scott's massive Bankside Power Station was transformed by architects Herzog & de Meuron into a gallery to house the Tate Gallery's collection of modern art. The new gallery opened in 2000 as Tate Modern, after which the Tate Gallery on Millbank (p.214) was rebranded as Tate Britain.

millennium bridge (2)
The Millennium Bridge was officially opened in May 2000 as the first new bridge to have opened in London since Tower Bridge in 1894. It was closed almost immediately due to the famous wobble and reopened in February 2002, £5m and 20 months later, with dampers to prevent the 'lozenge-pattern oscillation'.

shakespeare's globe (3)
In his prologue to King Henry V, Shakespeare asks **'may we cram within this wooden 'O' the very casques that did affright the air at Agincourt?'** – seen from the air it is easy to understand why he described his theatre as a wooden 'O'. This reconstruction, close to the site of the original Globe Theatre, opened in 1997 as the realization of a dream long-held by its founder, the late American actor and director Sam Wanamaker.

southwark bridge (4)
The present 5-arch steel bridge was built by Mott & Hay from 1912–21, to the designs of Sir Ernest George, to replace John Rennie's original cast-iron bridge (built 1814-19).
24'3"

alexandra bridge (5)
Alexandra Bridge, a 5-span plate girder construction better known as the Cannon Street Railway Bridge, was built from 1863–66 for the South Eastern Railway at the same time as Cannon Street Station and designed by the same architect, John Hawkshaw, with John Wolfe-Barry as engineer.

cannon st station (6)
Cannon Street Station was opened in 1866 with a spectacular single-span arched roof nearly 213 metres long and 30 metres high. The twin Baroque-style stone towers remain but Hawkshaw's roof was removed in 1958 and replaced during the 1960s with offices, shops and a roof garden over the tracks.

dock of st mary overie (7)
This dock, which was part of the Southwark Cathedral estate, now contains a replica of Sir Francis Drake's ship the **Golden Hind**. The original circumnavigated the globe from 1577–80; the replica was launched in 1973 and sailed round the world before being placed in permanent dock here.

LONDON BRIDGE TO TOWER PIER

Distance: 0.8 miles (1.3 kilometres)

Thames path: North bank – Following the embankment along the riverfront, with a detour around the Custom House (5). South bank – Rejoining the river east of London Bridge and then following the embankment along the riverfront.

southwark cathedral (1)

The very thing that provided the means for the foundation of Southwark Cathedral was almost its undoing – a Thames river crossing. Tradition has it that a convent was founded here in the 7th century and that the nuns obtained revenue from a ferry across the river (another version of the story is that the church and convent were built by a ferryman), but during the 19th century the chapel at the east end of the church was demolished to make way for John Rennie's new London Bridge. The church is dedicated to St Saviour & St Mary Overie; it was built between c. 1213-1520 and attained cathedral status in 1905.

london bridge (2)

The first London Bridge was built during the Roman occupation, and until 1729 London Bridge was the capital's only bridge across the river. The present 3-span concrete bridge was built from 1967-72 by Mott, Hay and Anderson with Lord Holford as architectural adviser. It replaced a bridge by John Rennie that now spans Lake Havasu in Arizona – legend has it that the purchasers thought they had bought Tower Bridge.
29'2"

hms belfast (3)

HMS Belfast's six-inch guns have a range of over fourteen miles, which would allow this Second World War cruiser to bombard Heston Services on the M4 or Scratchwood on the M1 from its current permanent mooring close to Tower Bridge. HMS Belfast was launched in 1938 as the largest cruiser ever built for the Royal Navy, was decommissioned after the Korean War and, since 1971, has been an annexe of the Imperial War Museum.

hay's galleria (4)

Built on the site of a narrow dock that was once part of the extensive Hay's Wharf (built in the mid-17th century by Alexander Hay), the Galleria is a piazza of shops and eating-places breathing fresh life into the space between the Victorian warehouses that lined the dock.

custom house (5)

The first Custom House was built in 1275 to the east of the present building. It was rebuilt several times after fires and a gunpowder explosion before a new, larger building was erected on the present site in 1813-17. Part of this new structure collapsed in 1825 and was rebuilt by Robert Smirke to give the building its present appearance – it was rebuilt to the original plans after damage during the Second World War

billingsgate market (6)

Billingsgate fish market dates from the 11th century. A purpose-built market hall was erected during the 1850s but soon proved inadequate, so Horace Jones designed the existing market hall, which was built from 1874-77 and is now a Grade II listed building. This building too eventually proved inadequate, and in 1982 the fish market moved to New Billinsgate Market on the Isle of Dogs (p.234).

Scale 1:3,125

225
up stream

fishmongers' hall

glazier's hall

6

5

tower pier

london bridge city pier

london bridge hospital

228 down stream

3

city hall (under construction)

4

london bridge station

tower pier

tower thistle hotel

227
up stream

city hall
(under construction)

st katharine's pier

upper pool
From London Bridge to Cherry
Garden Pier (p.230).

Scale 1:3,125

wapping high street

TOWER OF LONDON TO WAPPING

Distance: 0.8 miles (1.3 kilometres)
Thames path: North bank – Riverside, then
following Wapping High Street. South bank –
Following the embankment along the riverfront.

tower of london (1)

The Tower of London was first built by William the Conqueror c. 1067.
It is officially a royal palace, although it is far better known as a
prison – one American author even noted that the Tower "is to
poisoning, hanging, beheading, regicide and torture what the Yankee
Stadium is to baseball". The Tower's first prisoner was Ralf
Flambard, Bishop of Durham, who also one of the few to escape,
lowering a rope from a window after getting the guards drunk. The
last, 840 years later in 1941, was Rudolf Hess, although new evidence
implies that the man who then spent the rest of his life in Spandau
jail may have been an impostor and not the real Hess.

tower bridge (2)

Although it is only just over one hundred years old, Tower Bridge is,
with the possible exception of Big Ben, London's most famous
landmark, and is so closely identified with the capital that it is often
confused (in name, not profile) with London Bridge. Tower Bridge
was built from 1886–94 to the designs of architect Sir Horace Jones
and engineer John Wolfe-Barry. Designed to be in architectural harmony
with its ancient namesake, the Tower of London, the bridge has a stone-
clad steel frame to support the enormous weight of the lifting arms of
the roadway, known as bascules, from the French word for see-saw.
28'2"

st katharine docks (3)

The Royal Foundation of St Katharine was established here in 1148.
The Foundation's church survived the Reformation, the Great Fire of
London and the Gordon Riots only to be demolished in 1825 to make
way for the docks, which were designed by Thomas Telford and built
from 1827-28. Telford's revolutionary design of linked basins provided
an exceptional length of quayside for a relatively small enclosure of
water, while the warehouses were built close to the quayside to avoid
double handling of goods. The only surviving warehouse from
Telford's docks is the Ivory House, at the centre of the redeveloped
marina, which in its day handled not only ivory but also perfume,
wine and shells. Legend has it that the founder of a certain
multinational corporation used to collect discarded scallop shells
here, which years later provided him with the name and logo of his
organization, Shell Oil.

butler's wharf (4)

Like the surrounding Victorian warehouses, the 8-storey Butler's
Wharf warehouse from which the area takes its name has been
restored and converted into accommodation, shops and restaurants.
The area retains much of its Victorian atmosphere and was used by
David Lynch as a location for his film 'The Elephant Man'.

dickens inn (5)

Historic quayside inn, situated within St Katharine Docks

ST KATHARINE DOCKS TO LIMEHOUSE

Distance: 1.7 miles (2.8 kilometres)

Thames path: North bank – Wapping High Street, crossing Shadwell Pier Head and then following the riverfront. South bank – riverfront.

wapping pier head
The Pier Head that once served the Wapping Basin still exists, although the lock has been built over and the entrance is now a slipway. The Regency houses on the East and West Piers were built in 1811 as homes for officials of the London Dock Company.

former wapping basin
The curved edge of Wapping Sports Centre follows the outline of the former Wapping Basin, which provided the river entrance to the much larger, 20-acre Western Dock immediately to the north. Both were part of the London Docks, which were closed in 1969 and have since been filled and built over.

shadwell basin
Before closure in 1969, the London Docks covered more than 30 acres to the west of Shadwell Basin but most of the interlocking basins and docks have since been filled and built over. Shadwell Basin is the only part that still contains water, and it is now used as a yachting and canoeing activity centre.

tobacco dock
Alongside News International, the former warehouses of Tobacco Dock have been converted by Terry Farrell into a self-styled 'Covent Garden of Docklands' but the area remains eerily quiet because the enterprise went bust before it got off the ground. The dock itself is now a dry dock housing two sailing ships.

st katharine docks

news international

wapping high street

cherry garden pier

mayflower

Scale 1:6,250

ROTHERHITHE

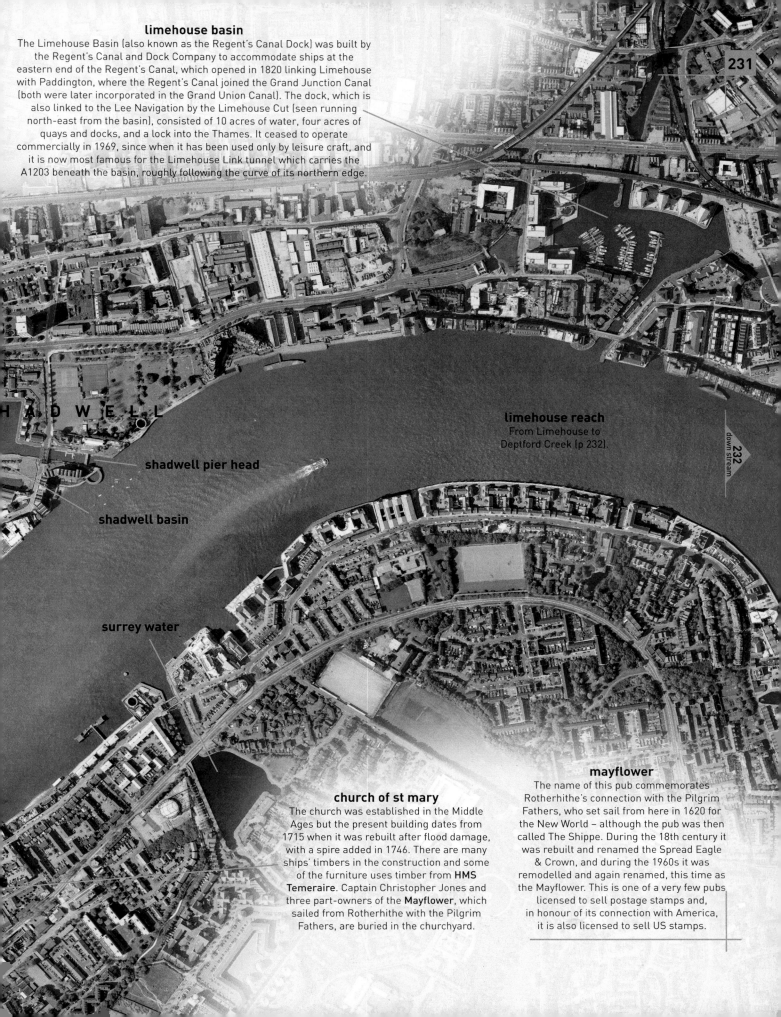

limehouse basin

The Limehouse Basin (also known as the Regent's Canal Dock) was built by the Regent's Canal and Dock Company to accommodate ships at the eastern end of the Regent's Canal, which opened in 1820 linking Limehouse with Paddington, where the Regent's Canal joined the Grand Junction Canal (both were later incorporated in the Grand Union Canal). The dock, which is also linked to the Lee Navigation by the Limehouse Cut (seen running north-east from the basin), consisted of 10 acres of water, four acres of quays and docks, and a lock into the Thames. It ceased to operate commercially in 1969, since when it has been used only by leisure craft, and it is now most famous for the Limehouse Link tunnel which carries the A1203 beneath the basin, roughly following the curve of its northern edge.

SHADWELL

limehouse reach
From Limehouse to Deptford Creek (p 232).

232 down stream

shadwell pier head

shadwell basin

surrey water

mayflower
The name of this pub commemorates Rotherhithe's connection with the Pilgrim Fathers, who set sail from here in 1620 for the New World – although the pub was then called The Shippe. During the 18th century it was rebuilt and renamed the Spread Eagle & Crown, and during the 1960s it was remodelled and again renamed, this time as the Mayflower. This is one of a very few pubs licensed to sell postage stamps and, in honour of its connection with America, it is also licensed to sell US stamps.

church of st mary
The church was established in the Middle Ages but the present building dates from 1715 when it was rebuilt after flood damage, with a spire added in 1746. There are many ships' timbers in the construction and some of the furniture uses timber from **HMS Temeraire**. Captain Christopher Jones and three part-owners of the **Mayflower**, which sailed from Rotherhithe with the Pilgrim Fathers, are buried in the churchyard.

231
up stream

canary wharf
(see pages
234–235)

blackwall reac

south dock

**westferry
road**

(thames path)

**greenland
dock**

millwall dock

mudchute

**millwall
park**

island gardens

**forest
products
terminal**

greenwich
(see pages
236–237)

Scale 1:12,500

D E P T F O R D

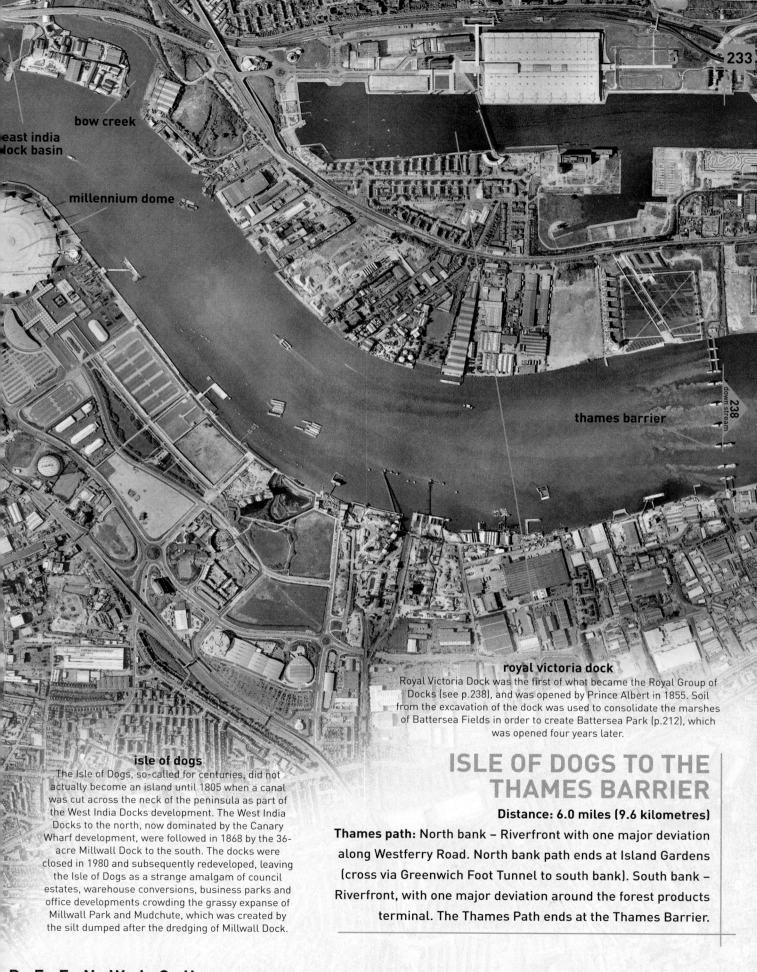

bow creek

east india
dock basin

millennium dome

thames barrier

238
down stream

royal victoria dock
Royal Victoria Dock was the first of what became the Royal Group of Docks (see p.238), and was opened by Prince Albert in 1855. Soil from the excavation of the dock was used to consolidate the marshes of Battersea Fields in order to create Battersea Park (p.212), which was opened four years later.

isle of dogs
The Isle of Dogs, so-called for centuries, did not actually become an island until 1805 when a canal was cut across the neck of the peninsula as part of the West India Docks development. The West India Docks to the north, now dominated by the Canary Wharf development, were followed in 1868 by the 36-acre Millwall Dock to the south. The docks were closed in 1980 and subsequently redeveloped, leaving the Isle of Dogs as a strange amalgam of council estates, warehouse conversions, business parks and office developments crowding the grassy expanse of Millwall Park and Mudchute, which was created by the silt dumped after the dredging of Millwall Dock.

ISLE OF DOGS TO THE THAMES BARRIER
Distance: 6.0 miles (9.6 kilometres)
Thames path: North bank – Riverfront with one major deviation along Westferry Road. North bank path ends at Island Gardens (cross via Greenwich Foot Tunnel to south bank). South bank – Riverfront, with one major deviation around the forest products terminal. The Thames Path ends at the Thames Barrier.

234

west india dock

billingsgate market

south dock

millwall dock

london arena

CANARY WHARF AND THE MILLENNIUM DOME

canary wharf development

The redevelopment of Canary Wharf on the former West India Dock is the largest office development ever to have taken place in London, providing the equivalent of one-seventh of all the office space in the City in 1987 when it was begun. The three landmark towers, visible from as far afield as Kent and Essex, form the grand centrepiece of the development, which also includes acres of lower-rise office buildings and Westferry Circus, a roundabout as big as Trafalgar Square. The name of the development derives from the fact that tomatoes and bananas were once landed here from the Canary Islands.

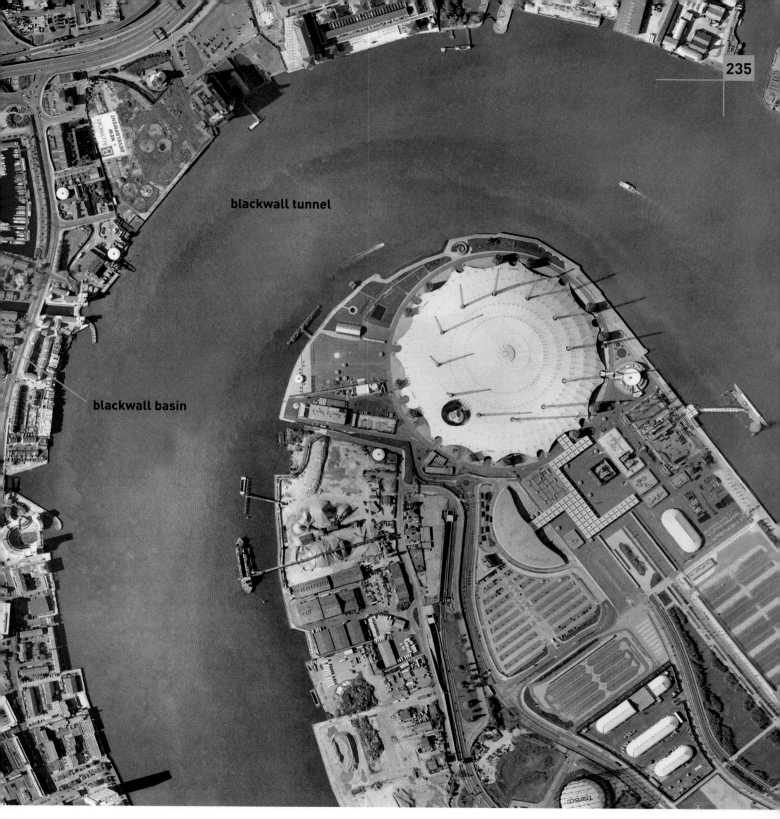

blackwall tunnel

blackwall basin

blackwall tunnel

The two bores of the Blackwall
Tunnel provide a major river crossing
at this point, the first of them built by
Sir Alexander Binnie in 1897. The
southbound tunnel, opened in 1967,
passes beneath the western edge of
the Dome, an airshaft destroying the
symmetry of the canopy.

millennium dome

Championed by the Tory government and vehemently opposed by the Labour
opposition, the Millennium Dome, designed by Richard Rogers, was causing
controversy before construction even began. When Labour swept to power the
controversy continued, with the Dome now championed by the Labour government
and vehemently opposed by the Tory opposition. Rock and roll lighting designer
Patrick Woodroffe lit the Dome in a different colour each night of the week during the
year 2000, an apt metaphor for the chameleon-like way in which the politicians dealt
with the question of how to celebrate the arrival of the new millennium.

GREENWICH

greenwich foot tunnel (1)
The circular entrance building provides access to the Greenwich Foot Tunnel, which was designed by Sir Alexander Binnie and opened on 4 August 1902. The tunnel is 1,217 feet long and c. 50 feet deep.

cutty sark (2)
Named after the short shift, or dress, worn by the witch Nannie in Robert Burns's poem 'Tam O'Shanter', **Cutty Sark** was launched in 1869 and made its name as a wool clipper. This famous ship was placed in dry dock here in 1954, and opened to the public in 1957.

gipsy moth iv (3)
This is the tiny 54 foot ketch in which, from 1966–67, Sir Francis Chichester became the first Englishman to sail around the world single-handed. On his return, Chichester was knighted by Queen Elizabeth II using the same sword that Queen Elizabeth I had used nearly 400 years earlier to knight Francis Drake for his circumnavigation.

royal naval college (4)
The former Royal Naval College, designed by Sir Christopher Wren and built from 1696-1742, was originally a naval hospital corresponding to the army's Chelsea Hospital. The Royal Naval College occupied the buildings from 1873 until 1997, after which they became part of the University of Greenwich. Wren's creation stands at the heart of the Maritime Greenwich World Heritage Site, so designated by UNESCO in recognition of the fact that this part of Greenwich comprises 'the finest and most dramatically sited architectural and landscape ensemble in the British Isles'.

national maritime museum (5)
Housed in the west wing of the former Royal Naval Asylum, the new-look National Maritime Museum reopened in time for Greenwich's millennium celebrations after a £20m refit.

queen's house (6)
Architect Inigo Jones was commissioned to build Queen's House for Anne of Denmark, the wife of James I, but she died in 1619 before it was completed. Building stopped until Jones was asked to complete it for Charles I's queen, Henrietta Maria. Originally H-shaped, the hose straddled what was then the Deptford-Woolwich road in order to give access to both the park and the river, the north and south wings being linked by a bridge. In 1662 John Webb added two first floor rooms over the road, closing the sides of the 'H' and creating the shape seen here; the road was diverted to its present position in 1697. The colonnades and wings were added in 1809 to accomodate the Royal Naval Asylum, which moved to Suffolk in 1933, after which Queen's House became part of the National Maritime Museum.

greenwich park (7)
In 1426, Humphrey, Duke of Gloucester, built himself a palatial mansion on the riverside at Greenwich, and seven years later he was given permission by Henry VI to enclose the 196 acres of land that now form Greenwich Park. It is the oldest of London's royal parks, and was opened to the public during the 18th century.

royal observatory (8)
Charles II's Royal Observatory in Greenwich Park is the country's longest-established scientific institution, set up in 1675 with the aim of solving by astronomy the problem of calculating longitude at sea. In the end the answer lay in being able to know the time at a given place, known as the Prime Meridian – the Greenwich Meridian, defined by the Observatory, was officially accepted as the Prime Meridian at an international conference in 1884.

Scale 1:3,125

SILVERTOWN TO CREEKMOUTH
Distance: 3.6 miles (5.8 kilometres)

thames barrier
This flood barrier was built from 1975–82, and at the official opening ceremony in 1984 the Queen described it as the Eighth Wonder of the World. Most of it is hidden under water: between the gleaming machine housings are ten retractable steel gates which lie in concrete sills on the river bed and take about 30 minutes to raise.

royal group of docks
The first of the Royal Group to be built was the Royal Victoria, to the west. It was such a success that it was extended to the east to form the Royal Albert Dock, the largest of the group. King George V Dock was begun in 1912 but the First World War delayed the work and it was not opened until 1921. In 1981, only 60 years after the last of the Royal Group opened, all three were closed, and later provided the site for City Airport.

silvertown
The name may seem overly romantic for such an industrial part of the riverside but it is not as fanciful as it seems: the area was first developed in the 1850s around the rubber and telegraph works of S. W. Silver & Co. Later, Henry Tate and Abram Lyle both opened sugar refineries here within a mile of each other in the late 19th century; the companies merged in 1921 and the main Tate & Lyle refinery is still at Silvertown.

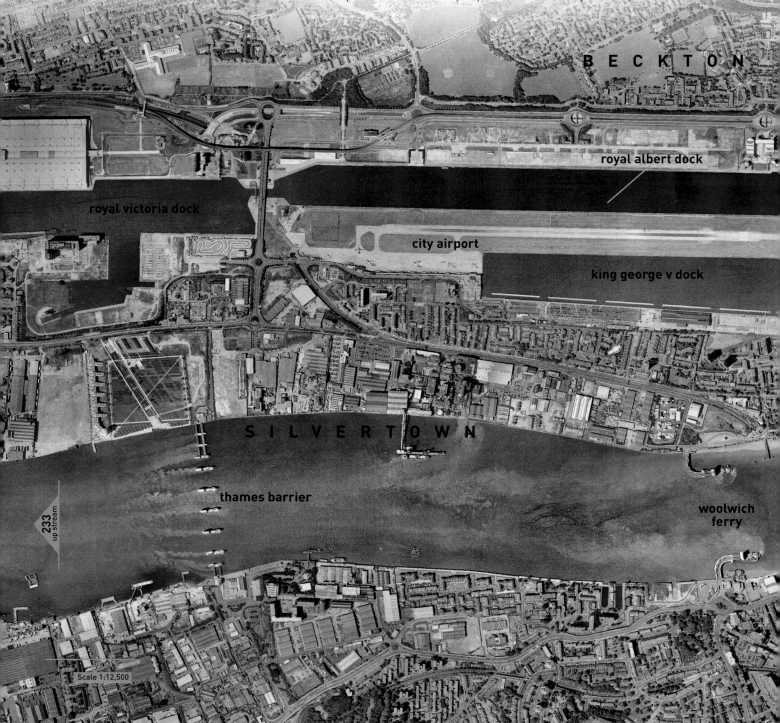

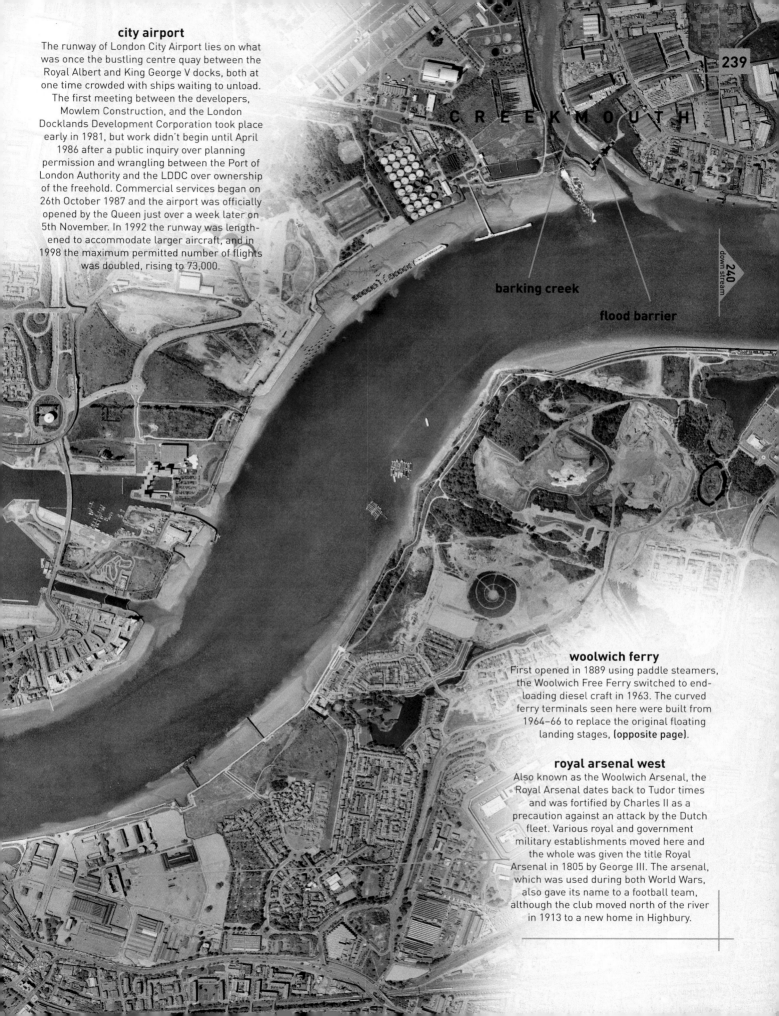

CREEKMOUTH

240
down stream

city airport

The runway of London City Airport lies on what was once the bustling centre quay between the Royal Albert and King George V docks, both at one time crowded with ships waiting to unload. The first meeting between the developers, Mowlem Construction, and the London Docklands Development Corporation took place early in 1981, but work didn't begin until April 1986 after a public inquiry over planning permission and wrangling between the Port of London Authority and the LDDC over ownership of the freehold. Commercial services began on 26th October 1987 and the airport was officially opened by the Queen just over a week later on 5th November. In 1992 the runway was lengthened to accommodate larger aircraft, and in 1998 the maximum permitted number of flights was doubled, rising to 73,000.

barking creek

flood barrier

woolwich ferry

First opened in 1889 using paddle steamers, the Woolwich Free Ferry switched to end-loading diesel craft in 1963. The curved ferry terminals seen here were built from 1964–66 to replace the original floating landing stages, (opposite page).

royal arsenal west

Also known as the Woolwich Arsenal, the Royal Arsenal dates back to Tudor times and was fortified by Charles II as a precaution against an attack by the Dutch fleet. Various royal and government military establishments moved here and the whole was given the title Royal Arsenal in 1805 by George III. The arsenal, which was used during both World Wars, also gave its name to a football team, although the club moved north of the river in 1913 to a new home in Highbury.

239
up stream

barking point
Also known as False Point.

cross ness

T H A M E S M E A D

thamesmead
Construction of this award-winning
new town began in 1967, planned by
the architects of the Greater London
Council.

sewag
works

erith mars

BARKING POINT TO
JENNINGTREE POINT

Distance: 3.3 miles (5.3 kilometres)

Scale 1:12,500

ford motor
works

jenningtree point

ford motor works

Henry Ford's son Edsel cut the first sod of earth for the new works at Dagenham in
May 1929, and the first vehicle (a model AA truck) was driven off the production line
17 months later in October 1931. In May 2000 Ford announced that it was to end
vehicle assembly at Dagenham and in February 2002 the last car rolled off the line
(a Fiesta, auctioned for charity), marking the end of an era after the assembly of
10,980,368 vehicles. Dagenham's new role is as Ford's main centre for the engineering
and manufacture of diesel engines, and a new engine plant due to be completed in
2003 will increase production to 900,000 engines per year.

242

frog island

241
up stream

rainham marshes

E R I T H

Scale 1:12,500

FROG ISLAND TO PURFLEET

Distance: 3.5 miles (5.7 kilometres)

hington marshes

aveley
marshes

purfleet rifle ranges

PURFLEET

crayford ness

river darent

river darent
flood barrier

river darent flood barrier

dartford marshes

sewage works

river darent

purfleet thames
terminal

littlebrook
power station

queen elizabeth II bridge

The last bridge on the Thames in two senses, the Queen
Elizabeth II bridge is the last downstream as well as being
chronologically the last road bridge to be built over the
tidal Thames (1988–91). When it was completed it was
Europe's largest cable-supported bridge, high enough for
the tallest liners to pass under the 54-metre-high, 450-
metre-wide central span. It cost £86 million to build,
raised by eight private companies, and is budgeted to pay
for itself through tolls over 14–20 years. The bridge has an
overall length of more than two miles and carries the
southbound carriageway of the M25 – northbound traffic
uses the two Dartford tunnels, which pass beneath the
Thames immediately upstream of the bridge.

littlebrook
nature park

DARTFORD MARSHES TO
WEST THURROCK MARSHES

Distance: 3.0 miles (4.9 kilometres)

Scale 1:12,500

west thurrock
marshes

queen
elizabeth II
bridge

246
down stream

ne
shes

245
up stream

broadness
salt marsh

swanscombe
marshes

botany
marshes

WEST THURROCK MARSHES
TO TILBURY DOCKS

Distance: 4.1 miles (6.6 kilometres)

Scale 1:12,500

tilbury docks

Tilbury occupied an important strategic position on the Thames long before the port was built here: the name itself, first recorded in the eighth century, refers to a stronghold or fortified place. The Port of Tilbury, constructed in 1888, covers an area of 800 acres and can handle ships of up to 12.5m draught and 304m length. It is a multi-purpose port handling in excess of 3,000 shipping movements per year, and includes the Northfleet Hope Terminal (to the west of the site), London's largest container terminal.

T I L B U R Y

tilbury ness

part of
tilbury docks

foot and
motorcycle
ferry

247
up stream

pocahontas memorial
The Native American princess Pocahontas is buried in the chancel of St George's
parish church in Gravesend, and a bronze memorial statue stands in the churchyard.
In 1608 Pocahontas saved the life of English settler Captain John Smith by placing
her head over his as a tomahawk was raised to execute him. She later married a
settler named John Rolfe who brought her to England in 1616, where she was fêted
at the court of James I, but she died of a fever the following year off Gravesend, while
sailing down the Thames to start her journey home to Virginia.

GRAVESEND
Distance: 1.6 miles (2.5 kilometres)

Scale 1:6,250

tilbury fort

Tilbury Fort, designed by Charles II's Chief Engineer Sir Bernard de Gomme to prevent the Dutch or French from entering London via the Thames, is celebrated as the finest and best-preserved example of 17th-century military engineering in the country. It was built in 1682 on the site of an earlier fort dating back to the reign of Henry VIII. Tilbury Fort is currently maintained by English Heritage.

THE THAMES ESTUARY

**Distance to Southend pier: 26.7 miles
(43.0 kilometres)**

STANFORD LE HOPE

THAMES HAVEN

249
up stream

GRAVESEND

Scale 1:200,000

LEIGH-ON-SEA

SOUTHEND-ON-SEA

CANVEY ISLAND

southend pier

ISLE OF GRAIN

river medway

INDEX